About the Cover Art

Cover Design: John Bell Art
<u>SelfPubBookCovers.com/JohnBellArt</u>[1]

---

1.   http://selfpubbookcovers.com/JohnBellArt

Management 101: Managing for Our Times

Management 101, Volume 1

David C. Wyld

Published by Sydney Gap Press, 2024.

While every precaution has been taken in the preparation of this book, the publisher assumes no responsibility for errors or omissions, or for damages resulting from the use of the information contained herein.

MANAGEMENT 101: MANAGING FOR OUR TIMES

First edition. June 1, 2024.

ISBN: 979-8224084166

Written by David C. Wyld.

Also by David C. Wyld

Management 101
Management 101: Managing for Our Times

Watch for more at https://www.linkedin.com/in/
david-wyld-4923707/.

Table of Contents

For Mom...

Preface

This book is the first in a series of *"Management 101"* books. There are several reasons why I felt compelled to start this series of books. The first is topical. As a management professor for now three decades-plus, one of the things that I see is that all too often, we over-rely on the "tried and true" models of managing that serve as the current basis for much of management education and training, even though much of "management thought" hails from the 1920s, '30s, '50s and '70s! Heck, 1980s and '90s stuff is considered "modern" still today by many in the field!

But there's a whole new world of management ideas, and this is what I want to open your eyes to what are some of the emerging and really cutting-edge ideas out there. Unprecedented times call for unprecedented models and ideas for managing people and businesses. And this is precisely what this series aims to do: Give you the latest tools in management. So, I really hope that you will enjoy - get a whole lot out of this book!

The second reason behind starting this book series is practical. One of the things about us professors is that we tend to write a whole lot that "normal" people NEVER see. The thing that brings us the most prestige and most reward is to write journal articles that appear in academic journals that, well, only gather dust on library shelves - or these days - no downloads. A few years back, I made the call to aim my work at wider audiences through more accessible trade journal-type outlets. That has been a career altering decision, as now I write for the masses, rather than for the few. And I have been overwhelmed at the response and feedback my articles have garnered online. This then is the first collection of my articles written for Medium - and for their

Modern Business and Management Now publications, and with this book, I hope to start reaching out to a whole new audience for my work.

Now, I have listened for many years, first on the radio and now to his podcast, to Tony Kornheiser, a former Washington, DC-based sportswriter that many of you know from the *"PTI"* show on ESPN. In 2002, "Mr. Tony" published a book that was a collection of his newspaper columns with the catchiest - *and* most honest - book title you could ever see for a compilation book. It was titled, *"I'm Back for More Cash: Because You Can't Take Two Hundred Newspapers into the Bathroom!"* I am now merely following in his footsteps with a compilation book of my own management articles. So, yes, this book is also a practical way for you to consume my work, while also being a way for you to support the author by buying this ebook!

Please look for future entires in the "Management 101" series. I look forward to engaging with you and hearing your feedback! You can contact me anytime via email at dwyld@selu.edu. I very much look forward to hearing from you!

Now, sit back and enjoy the book! I'm very glad - and honored - to have you here to read my work! If you enjoy it, please leave me a good review and pass this ebook on to your friends, colleagues, and maybe even your boss!

Chapter 1

MBWA Means Getting Your Steps In as a Manager

Why Managing by Wandering Around is the One Management Technique Every Manager Needs to Do Today

Overview

MBWA, or managing by wandering around, is a management technique that emphasizes the importance of a manager being present and involved in the day-to-day activities of their team. The idea behind MBWA (which alternatively can stand for *"Managing by Walking Around"*) is that a manager who is present and involved can better understand the needs and concerns of their team and can make more informed decisions as a result.

To put it simply, MBWA involves a manager getting out of their office and spending time with their team, observing their work, and engaging in conversations with them. This technique can be particularly effective in environments where teamwork is essential, employees are highly skilled, and communication is critical.

In this chapter, we will explore the benefits of MBWA—beyond just getting your steps in—look at how to implement it, and explore some best practices for getting the most out of this management technique.

The Origins of MBWA

The concept of MBWA, or managing by wandering around, was first introduced by Tom Peters and Robert Waterman in their book "In Search of Excellence" in 1982. Peters and Waterman were consultants at McKinsey & Company, and they studied successful companies to identify common traits that contributed to their success.

During their research, Peters and Waterman observed that successful leaders were often highly visible and engaged with their teams. They spent time on the front lines, observing work, engaging in conversations, and providing feedback. They found that this approach helped leaders better understand their teams' needs and concerns and make more informed decisions as a result.

Peters and Waterman coined the term "managing by wandering around" to describe this management style. They argued that it effectively improved communication and collaboration, boosted employee engagement, and enhanced problem-solving and decision-making.

The MBWA idea quickly gained popularity, and it has since been embraced by many organizations and managers around the world. While the term itself may be somewhat informal, the principles behind MBWA are sound and have been shown to be effective in a wide range of industries and contexts.

Benefits of MBWA

There are several benefits to managing by wandering around. Some of the most notable include:

1. *Improved communication:* A manager can better understand their team's needs and concerns by spending time with their team and engaging in conversations with them. This, in turn, can lead to improved communication and more effective collaboration.

2. Increased employee engagement: When a manager is present and involved in their team's work, it can help to boost employee morale and engagement. This is because employees feel their work is important and their manager cares about their success.

3. Enhanced problem-solving: By observing their team's work, a manager can identify potential issues or inefficiencies and take action to address them. This can lead to more effective problem-solving and a more productive team.

4. Improved decision-making: By having a better understanding of their team's work, a manager can make more informed decisions about resource allocation, project management, and other key areas.

Implementing MBWA

Implementing MBWA is relatively straightforward. Here are some steps to follow:

1. Schedule regular check-ins: Set aside time on a regular basis to check in with your team. This could be a daily or weekly check-in, depending on the size of your team and the nature of your work.

2. Observe your team's work: Spend time observing your team's work and processes. This will help you better understand how they work and identify potential areas for improvement.

3. Engage in conversations: Take the time to engage in conversations with your team members. Ask them about their work, their concerns, and their ideas for improving processes or workflows.

4. Provide feedback: Offer feedback to your team members on their work. This can help to boost morale and engagement, and can also help to identify areas where additional training or support may be needed.

Best Practices for MBWA

To get the most out of Managing by Wandering Around, there are some best practices to keep in mind when engaging in your intentional wandering. These include:

1. Be present: When you're engaging in MBWA, make sure to be fully present and engaged with your team. This means putting away your phone and other distractions and focusing on the conversation at hand.

2. Be open-minded: Keep an open mind and be receptive to new ideas and feedback from your team. This can help to foster a culture of innovation and collaboration.

3. Encourage feedback: Encourage your team members to provide feedback on their work and the processes they use. This can help to identify areas for improvement and can also help to boost engagement and morale.

4. Follow-up: After engaging in MBWA, make sure to follow up with your team members on any feedback or ideas that were discussed. This can help to demonstrate that you value their input and are committed to improving processes and workflows.

Conclusion

Managing by wandering around can be a highly effective management technique, particularly in environments where communication and collaboration are critical. By being present and engaged with their team, managers can better understand their needs and concerns, improve communication and cooperation, and make more informed decisions. By following best practices for MBWA, managers can get the most out of this management technique and help to create a more productive and engaged team.

If you're interested in implementing MBWA in your management style, here are some steps you can take to get started:

1. Assess your current management style: Take some time to reflect on your current management style. Are you spending enough time with your team? Do you feel disconnected from their daily activities? Identifying areas for improvement can help you to understand better why MBWA may be a good fit for your team.

2. Schedule regular check-ins: Set aside time on a regular basis to check in with your team. This could be a daily or weekly check-in, depending on the size of your team and the nature of your work.

3. Observe your team's work: Spend time observing your team's work and processes. This will help you to understand better how they work and identify potential areas for improvement.

4. Engage in conversations: Take the time to engage in conversations with your team members. Ask them about their work, their concerns, and their ideas for improving processes or workflows.

5. Provide feedback: Offer feedback to your team members on their work. This can help boost morale and engagement and identify areas where additional training or support may be needed.

6. Follow up: After engaging in MBWA, make sure to follow up with your team members on any feedback or ideas that were discussed. This can help to demonstrate that you value their input and are committed to improving processes and workflows.

7. Be consistent: Consistency is key when implementing MBWA. Make sure to set aside time on a regular basis to engage in MBWA with your team and follow through on any feedback or ideas that were discussed.

Implementing MBWA may require some adjustments to your current management style, but the benefits can be significant. By being present and engaged with your team, you can improve communication and collaboration, boost employee engagement, and make more informed decisions - and yes, get those steps in, too!

Chapter 2
Managing for Creativity
How to inspire creativity in your work teams to produce better results

Overview

As a manager, one of your responsibilities is to inspire creativity in your work team. Creativity is essential in any business as it drives innovation, improves problem-solving, and creates opportunities for growth. Encouraging creativity in your team can lead to new ideas, improved processes, and better outcomes. However, inspiring creativity requires more than just asking your team to be creative. In this chapter, we'll explore some tips for inspiring creativity in your work team.

How Managers Can Inspire Creativity in Their Work Teams

1. Set clear goals and expectations

One of the first things you can do as a manager is to set clear goals and expectations for your team. When your team knows what they need to accomplish, they can focus their creative energy on finding innovative solutions to achieve those goals. Be sure to communicate your expectations clearly and provide your team with the resources and support they need to achieve them.

2. Encourage brainstorming sessions

Brainstorming sessions can be a great way to get your team thinking creatively. Encourage your team to share their ideas, no matter how unconventional they may seem. Make sure everyone has a chance to speak and that all ideas are heard and considered.

3. Foster an open and inclusive culture

Creating a culture that encourages open communication and inclusivity can also inspire creativity in your team. Encourage your team to share their ideas and opinions, no matter how unconventional they may be. Be sure to listen actively to their suggestions and provide constructive feedback. When your team feels heard and valued, they are more likely to take risks and think outside the box.

4. Provide opportunities for learning and growth

Providing opportunities for learning and growth can also inspire creativity in your team. Encourage your team to attend conferences, workshops, and training sessions to learn new skills and gain new perspectives. You can also provide opportunities for job shadowing or mentorship programs to help your team members learn from one another. When your team members feel that they are growing professionally, they are more likely to bring new ideas and approaches to their work.

5. Provide resources and tools

Make sure your team has the resources and tools they need to be creative. This can include access to software, equipment, or even just a space to work. Providing these resources can show your team that you are invested in their success.

6. Encourage collaboration and teamwork

Collaboration and teamwork can also inspire creativity in your team. Encourage your team members to work together on projects and share their ideas and perspectives. You can also create cross-functional teams to encourage collaboration across different departments. When your team members work together, they can build on each other's strengths and come up with more creative solutions.

7. Lead by example

As a manager, it's important to lead by example. Show your team that you value creativity by being creative yourself. Share your ideas and encourage collaboration. This can help inspire your team to be more creative as well.

8. Embrace experimentation and risk-taking

Finally, as a manager, you can inspire creativity by embracing experimentation and risk-taking. Encourage your team members to try new things and take calculated risks. When your team members feel that they have the freedom to experiment and take risks, they are more likely to come up with innovative ideas and solutions. Be sure to celebrate your team's successes, even when their experiments don't go as planned.

Conclusion

Inspiring creativity in your work team requires a combination of clear goals and expectations, an open and inclusive culture, opportunities for learning and growth, collaboration and teamwork, and experimentation and risk-taking. When you foster a creative environment in your team, you can drive innovation and improve your business outcomes. As a manager, it's your responsibility to inspire and motivate your team to be creative and innovative in their work.

Chapter 3

The Power of Listening to Customers

In short, listening - really listening to customers - pays big dividends for businesses that make the effort to do so.

Overview

In today's competitive business environment, management needs to understand the needs and expectations of their customers more than ever. By listening to their customers, management can gain valuable insights to help them improve their products and services, increase customer satisfaction, and ultimately drive business growth and success.

The Importance of Listening to Customers

One of the key benefits of listening to customers is that it helps management to understand their needs and expectations. This is essential for creating products and services that meet customers' needs. According to a study by Bain & Company, companies that listen to their customers and act on their feedback grow revenue 2-3 times faster than their competitors! So, the bottom line is that listening pays - *big!*

Another important benefit of listening to customers is that it helps to build stronger relationships with them. When customers feel that they are being heard and that their opinions matter, they are more likely to develop a sense of loyalty towards the company. This can lead to repeat business, positive word-of-mouth referrals, and increased customer lifetime value.

Listening to customers can also help management to identify potential issues before they become major problems. By monitoring customer feedback and addressing issues in a timely manner, management can prevent small problems from turning into larger ones that can damage the company's reputation.

How to Listen to Customers

Listening to customers is not just about hearing what they say; it's about understanding their needs and expectations. Here are some tips for REALLY listening to customers:

1. Use multiple channels: Customers may prefer to provide feedback through different channels such as email, phone, social media, or in-person. By providing multiple channels for feedback, management can ensure that they capture feedback from as many customers as possible.

2. Ask for feedback: Rather than waiting for customers to provide feedback, management can proactively ask for it. This can be done through surveys, focus groups, or other feedback mechanisms.

3. Respond to feedback: It's not enough to just listen to customers, management also needs to respond to their feedback. This can be done by addressing issues, improving products or services, or simply thanking customers for their feedback.

4. Act on feedback: In order to truly benefit from listening to customers, management needs to act on their feedback. This can involve making changes to products or services, improving customer service, or addressing issues that are causing dissatisfaction.

5. Monitor feedback: Listening to customers is an ongoing process. Management needs to monitor customer feedback and make adjustments as needed continuously.

Conclusion

Listening to customers is essential for management to understand their needs and expectations, build stronger relationships, and identify potential issues before they become major problems. By using multiple feedback channels, proactively asking for feedback, responding to feedback, acting on feedback, and continuously monitoring feedback, management can harness the power of listening to drive business growth and success.

Chapter 4

Why You Must Embrace the Chaos of the Change Process to Succeed

Applying the Satir Change Management Methodology to Managing Transitions in Companies Today

Overview

Managing change is a challenging task for any organization. In fact, for managers, it may be one of the most daunting - and yet important - things they do. Change can be unsettling and disruptive for employees, and it can be challenging to ensure that everyone is on board and working towards the same goals.

The Satir Change Management Methodology provides a framework for managing change and transition effectively. In this chapter, we will explore how the Satir model can be applied to management for managing organizational changes.

Figure 1: The Satir Change Management Model

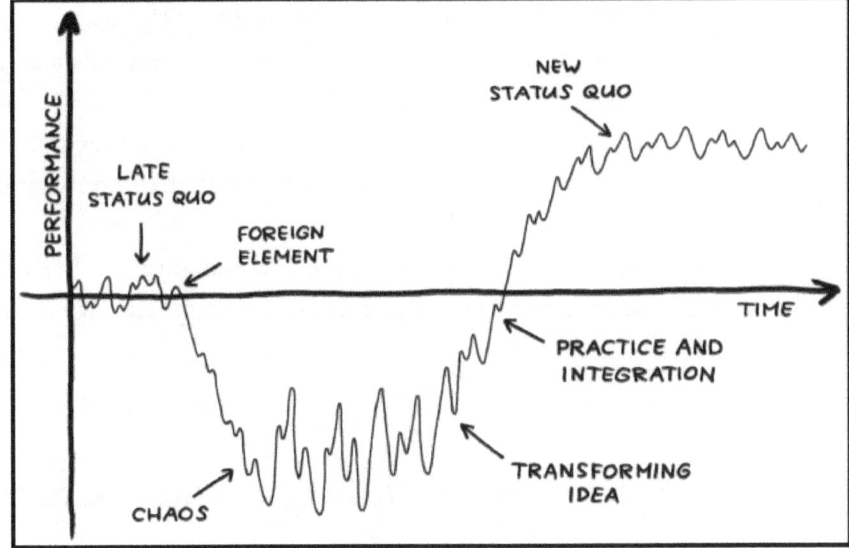

Source: Satir, Virginia et al. *The Satir Model.* Palo Alto: Science and Behavior Books, 1991. *(Used with permission).*

—————⊙—————

The Satir Change Management Methodology

The Satir Change Management Methodology was developed by Virginia Satir, a renowned family therapist and communication expert. This methodology is designed to help individuals, teams, and organizations manage change and transition effectively. The Satir Change Management Model *(see Figure 1 above)* consists of five stages:

1. Late Status Quo: This stage is characterized by a sense of comfort and familiarity with the current situation and a resistance to change.

2. Resistance: In this stage, individuals may feel fear, anxiety, or anger towards the change and may actively resist it (the foreign element).

3. Chaos: In this stage, the old ways of doing things have been disrupted, but the new ways have not yet been fully established. This can be a confusing and difficult stage.

4. Integration: In this stage, individuals begin to understand and accept the new situation and start to work together to establish new ways of doing things.

5. New Status Quo: In this final stage, the change has been fully integrated, and individuals feel comfortable and familiar with the new situation.

The Satir Methodology and Change Management

The Satir Change Management Methodology emphasizes the importance of communication, empathy, and collaboration throughout the change process. It is often used in organizational change management, but it can also be applied to personal or team-level changes.

Let's take a closer look at each stage and how it applies to management.

1. Late Status Quo

The Late Status Quo stage is characterized by a sense of comfort and familiarity with the current situation and a resistance to change. In a management context, this might mean that employees are comfortable with the way things are and are resistant to any changes that might be proposed.

To move through this stage, it is crucial to communicate clearly and openly with employees about why change is necessary. This might involve explaining the business reasons behind the change, outlining the benefits that the change will bring, and addressing any concerns that employees might have.

2. Resistance

In the Resistance stage, individuals may feel fear, anxiety, or anger towards the change, and may actively resist it. This can be a challenging stage for managers, as it can be difficult to overcome employees' resistance to change.

To move through this stage, it is vital to listen to employees' concerns and address them as best as possible. This might involve providing additional information or training to help employees feel more comfortable with the change or involving employees in the change process to give them a sense of ownership.

3. Chaos

In the Chaos stage, the old ways of doing things have been disrupted, but the new ways have not yet been fully established. This can be a confusing and challenging stage for both managers and employees.

To move through this stage, it is important to provide clear direction and support to employees. This might involve setting clear goals and expectations, providing additional training or resources to help employees adapt to the new situation, and being available to answer questions or provide guidance as needed.

4. Integration

In the Integration stage, individuals begin to understand and accept the new situation and start to work together to establish new ways of doing things. This is often the most productive stage of the change process, as employees are beginning to feel more comfortable with the change and are working together towards a common goal.

To move through this stage, it is essential to continue to provide support and guidance to employees. This might involve acknowledging their progress and achievements, providing ongoing training and resources to help them refine their skills, and encouraging collaboration and teamwork.

5. New Status Quo

In the New Status Quo stage, the change has been fully integrated, and individuals feel comfortable and familiar with the new situation. This is the final stage of the change process, and it is important to celebrate the achievement of this milestone.

To maintain the new status quo, it is vital to continue to support and develop employees. This might involve providing ongoing training and development opportunities, encouraging employees to share their ideas and feedback, and monitoring the success of the change to ensure that it is delivering the expected benefits.

Example of Implementing a New Software System

Let's say a company wants to implement a new software system across all departments. The first stage in the Satir model is the Late Status Quo, where the company recognizes the need for change. In this stage, the company identifies the current system's inefficiencies and decides to implement a new software system to streamline their operations.

The second stage is Resistance. Here, employees may resist the change, fearing that the new system will be difficult to use or disrupt their workflow. The company can address this by providing employees with training sessions, explaining the benefits of the new system, and involving them in the decision-making process.

The third stage is Chaos, which can occur during the implementation of the new system. During this phase, employees may experience confusion or frustration as they adjust to the new software. To minimize the impact of chaos, the company can provide ongoing support, such as a help desk or designated experts who can answer questions and provide guidance.

The fourth stage is Integration, where the new system becomes a part of the company's daily operations. To successfully integrate the system, the company can celebrate milestones, recognize employees who have adapted well, and provide ongoing training and support as needed.

Finally, the fifth stage is the New Status Quo, where the new system is fully integrated into the company's operations. In this stage, the company can evaluate the effectiveness of the new system by monitoring progress and soliciting feedback from employees.

***

Example of Implementing a New Performance Management Process

Let's say a company wants to implement a new performance management system for its employees. The Satir Change Management Methodology can be applied to help employees transition smoothly to this new system.

In the Late Status Quo stage, the company communicates the need for change to the employees and explains the benefits of the new performance management system. This helps employees understand why the change is necessary and what they can expect from the new system.

In the Resistance stage, employees may feel anxious or resistant to the new system. To overcome this resistance, the company can involve employees in the change process by providing training and resources to help them understand how the new system works. This can help employees feel more comfortable with the change and give them a sense of ownership in the process.

In the Chaos stage, the company can help employees adapt to the new system by providing support and guidance. This might involve setting clear goals and expectations, providing additional training or resources to help employees adapt to the new system, and being available to answer questions or provide guidance as needed.

In the Integration stage, employees begin to understand and accept the new system and start working together to establish new ways of working. The company can encourage collaboration and teamwork by creating opportunities for employees to share their ideas and feedback on the new system. This can help employees feel valued and engaged in the change process.

In the New Status Quo stage, the change has been fully integrated, and employees feel comfortable and familiar with the new performance management system. The company can celebrate this achievement by acknowledging the hard work and effort put in by employees to make the transition successful. To maintain the new status quo, the company can continue to support and develop employees by providing ongoing training and development opportunities and monitoring the success of the new system.

———◦———

Analysis

The Satir Change Management Methodology emphasizes the importance of communication, empathy, and collaboration throughout the change process. In a management context, this means that managers need to be open and transparent about why change is necessary and to be supportive and empathetic towards employees who may be struggling with the change.

It is also important for managers to involve employees in the change process, giving them a sense of ownership and control over the changes that are being made. This can help to reduce resistance to change and increase buy-in from employees.

———◦———

Conclusion

In conclusion, the Satir Change Management Methodology provides a helpful framework for managing change in a management context. By understanding and applying the five stages of the Satir model, managers can help to ensure that change is managed effectively and that employees can adapt to the new situation with minimal disruption.

Chapter 5
A Little Nudge Can Go a Long Way
How to give your employees the nudge they may need to change their ways

Overview

Nudge theory is a concept in behavioral economics that has gained popularity in recent years. Nudge theory suggests that indirect and subtle interventions can influence the behavior and decision-making of individuals. It proposes that small changes in the environment or the presentation of information can encourage people to make better choices without forcing them to do so. The idea is that by making certain choices easier or more attractive, people will be more likely to make them. This theory has been applied to various areas, such as public health, environmental conservation, and financial decision-making. However, it has also shown promising results in the field of management.

In this chapter, we will look at how nudge theory has been successfully applied in management and provide practical recommendations for managers to give their employees a nudge!

Nudge Theory in Management

Nudge theory has been applied in various management contexts, such as employee motivation, change management, and decision-making. The basic idea behind nudge theory is that small changes in the environment or the presentation of information can encourage people to make better choices without forcing them to do so. This approach is based on the assumption that people are not always rational and often make decisions based on heuristics and biases.

Employee Motivation

Nudge theory can be applied to motivate employees by making certain behaviors easier or more attractive. For example, a study conducted by the University of Warwick found that providing free fruit and vegetables in the workplace increased employee productivity by 10-12%. This intervention was based on the principle of convenience, as it made healthy food options more accessible and convenient for the employees.

Another example of nudge theory in employee motivation is the use of gamification. Gamification involves applying game design elements to non-game contexts, such as the workplace. This approach can be used to motivate employees by making work more engaging and fun. For instance, a study conducted by the University of Pennsylvania found that a gamified sales training program led to a 9% increase in sales.

Change Management

Nudge theory can also be applied to facilitate change management. Change management involves implementing changes in an organization to improve its performance or achieve specific goals. However, change management is often met with resistance from employees who are comfortable with the status quo. Nudge theory can be used to overcome this resistance by making the change more attractive or easier to adopt.

For example, a study conducted by the University of California, Berkeley found that changing the default printer settings from single-sided to double-sided led to a 40% reduction in paper usage. This intervention was based on the principle of defaults, as it made double-sided printing the default option, thus making it easier for employees to adopt the behavior.

Decision-Making

Nudge theory can also be applied to improve decision-making in an organization. Decision-making is a complex process that involves evaluating multiple options and choosing the best one. However, decision-making is often influenced by biases and heuristics that can lead to suboptimal choices. Nudge theory can be used to overcome these biases by presenting information in a way that promotes better decision-making.

For example, a study conducted by the University of Chicago found that presenting information about energy usage in terms of social norms (e.g., "90% of your neighbors use energy-efficient light bulbs") led to a 2.5-5% reduction in energy usage. This intervention was based on the principle of social norms, as it appealed to the desire to conform to the behavior of others.

Examples of Using Nudges in Organizations

Managers can use nudge theory to change employee behaviors in various ways. Some examples include:

1. Providing healthy snacks: Managers can nudge employees towards healthier eating habits by providing healthy snacks like fruits and vegetables instead of junk food. This can be done by placing fruit baskets in common areas or providing free healthy snacks in the break room.

2. *Changing default options:* Managers can change the default options on company software or equipment to encourage employees to make better choices. For example, setting the default printer options to print double-sided can encourage employees to use less paper.

3. *Gamification:* Managers can use gamification to nudge employees towards desired behaviors. This can be done by creating a game-like atmosphere in the workplace that engages employees and encourages them to complete certain tasks or meet specific goals.

4. Social norms: Managers can use social norms to nudge employees towards certain behaviors. For example, displaying posters or signs that highlight the behaviors of top-performing employees can encourage other employees to emulate them.

5. *Feedback*: Managers can use feedback to nudge employees towards better performance. This can be done by providing regular feedback on employee performance and offering suggestions for improvement.

Overall, nudge theory can be used by managers to encourage positive behaviors without using force or coercion. By understanding the principles of nudge theory, managers can create environments that promote positive behaviors and improve employee performance.

Recommendations for Managers to Use Nudges

The following list is a step-by-step process by which a manager can apply nudge theory to change employee behaviors and decision-making in the direction he or she might want for them

1. Identify the behavioral problem: Managers should first identify the specific behavior that they want to change or promote.

2. Understand the context: Managers should understand the context in which the behavior occurs, including the physical environment, social norms, and organizational culture.

3. Choose the appropriate nudge: Managers should choose the appropriate nudge based on the behavioral problem and the context. For example, if the goal is to promote healthy eating, providing free fruit and vegetables in the workplace may be an effective nudge.

4. Test the nudge: Managers should test the effectiveness of the nudge before implementing it on a larger scale. This can be done through pilot studies or experiments.

5. Monitor and adjust: Managers should monitor the effectiveness of the nudge and adjust it as necessary. This can be done through feedback from employees or data analysis.

Conclusion

Nudge theory is a powerful tool for managers to influence the behavior and decision-making of employees. By making small changes in the environment or the presentation of information, managers can promote desirable behaviors and overcome resistance to change. However, it is important to choose the appropriate nudge based on the behavioral problem and the context, and to test and monitor its effectiveness before implementing it on a larger scale.

Chapter 6
The Untold Story
The Employer's Guide to Interviewing

Overview

Interviewing candidates is a crucial step in the hiring process. It is the opportunity where employers can learn more about a candidate's skills, experience, and personality to determine if they would be a good fit for the company. However, interviewing can also be a daunting task for many employers. Not only do they need to assess the candidate's qualifications, but they also need to make a positive impression and represent their company in the best possible light. The latter is now essential in today's highly competitive job market, where good workers can - and do - choose where and for whom they want to work!

In this chapter, we will provide you with some tips on how to conduct successful interviews and hire the "right" candidates - the ones who will turn out to be good hires and good employees - for your organization. We will also provide you with a list of questions that can serve as a good starting point as you prepare to interview job candidates.

Steps for an Employer to Take in the Interview Process

Regardless of the circumstances, there aee some basic steps that you need to take on the employer side of the interview equation to make the process "work/" These include the following.

1. Prepare for the interview

Before the interview, make sure you have reviewed the candidate's resume and cover letter, as well as any other application materials they may have provided. This will help you identify any areas of concern or questions you may have before the interview. It is also a good idea to prepare a list of interview questions that are tailored to the specific job and company. This will help ensure you gather the necessary information to make an informed decision.

2. Create a welcoming atmosphere

Creating a welcoming atmosphere can help put the candidate at ease and make the interview process less stressful. Start by greeting the candidate warmly and offering them a comfortable place to sit. You can also offer them a drink or a snack if you have them available. Small gestures like these can help create a positive impression and show the candidate that you value their time and effort.

3. Be structured and organized

A structured and organized interview process can help ensure that you cover all the necessary topics and gather all the information you need to make a decision. Start by introducing yourself and the company, and then provide an overview of the interview process. This can help the candidate understand what to expect and how they can best prepare for the interview. Stick to the questions you have prepared, but be open to follow-up questions or additional information the candidate may provide.

4. Listen carefully

Listening carefully to the candidate's answers can help you gain a better understanding of their qualifications and experience. It can also help you identify any red flags or concerns that may need to be addressed. Take notes during the interview so you can refer back to them later when making your decision.

5. Ask behavioral questions

Behavioral questions are a type of interview question that asks the candidate to provide examples of how they have handled specific situations in the past. These questions can help you assess the candidate's problem-solving skills, communication skills, and ability to work well with others. Examples of behavioral questions include:

- Can you tell me about a time when you had to deal with a difficult customer?

- Can you describe a situation where you had to work with a team to achieve a common goal?

- Can you give an example of how you have demonstrated leadership in a previous role?

6. Sell the company

The interview process is not just an opportunity for you to assess the candidate; it is also an opportunity for the candidate to learn more about your company and the job. Take the time to sell your company and the job by highlighting its benefits, culture, and growth opportunities. This can help the candidate understand why your company is a great place to work and why they should want to join your team.

7. Follow up

After the interview, follow up with the candidate to let them know where they stand in the hiring process. Whether you decide to move forward with the candidate or not, it is important to provide them with feedback and closure. This can help maintain a positive relationship with the candidate, even if they are not the right fit for the job.

What Questions Should You Ask of Prospective Employees?

For anyone involved in the hiring process, one of the most important tasks they have is to develop a list of questions to ask interviewees. The following is a suggested "starter" list of questions that you can use as the basis for conducting an interview. Of course, you should customize your list of questions to match the situation - but the most important thing is to have an actual list of questions! In other words, don't try and simply "wing it!" Improving an interview really is not a good idea, as it is not a good way for you to get to know the person you are interviewing or to make a good impression on the job candidate!

1. Can you tell me about your previous work experience in this field?

2. What motivated you to apply for this position?

3. How do you handle stressful situations at work?

4. Can you give an example of a time when you had to work with a difficult team member?

5. What are your long-term career goals?

6. How do you stay up-to-date with industry trends and developments?

7. Can you describe a work-related challenge you faced and how you overcame it?

8. What skills or qualities do you possess that make you a good fit for this position?

9. Can you tell me about a time when you had to make a difficult decision at work?

10. How do you prioritize your work and manage your time effectively?

11. What are your goals for the future, and how do you see this position helping you achieve them?

12. What questions do you have for me - about the job, the company, or anything else?

———◦———

Conclusion

In sum, conducting successful interviews is a *critical* part of the hiring process. By preparing for the interview, creating a welcoming atmosphere, being structured and organized, listening carefully, asking behavioral questions, selling the company, and following up, employers can increase their chances of hiring the right candidate for the job. Good luck with your interviews - and like a Boy Scout, remember to, above all, "be prepared!"

Chapter 7

Making the Eisenhower Matrix Work for You Today

An overview of this great tool for prioritizing the importance and urgency of tasks and planning your schedule based on the true criticality of everything on your "to do" list.

"I have two kinds of problems, the urgent and the important. The urgent are not important, and the important are never urgent." -Dwight D. Eisenhower, 34th U.S. President

Overview

The *Eisenhower Matrix* - also referred to as the *Urgent-Important Matrix* - is a time-management tool that helps people prioritize tasks based on their level of importance and urgency. The matrix is a simple yet effective tool that can help you organize your work and personal life, allowing you to be more productive and achieve your goals. It is named after former U.S. President Dwight D. Eisenhower, who was known for his ability to manage his time effectively. Oh, and by the way, he planned and led a little thing called D-Day in World War II.

In this chapter, we will explore how you can use the Eisenhower Matrix to your advantage in your career. We will discuss what the matrix is, how it works, and how you can apply it to your daily routine to become more productive and efficient.

Figure 1 - The Eisenhower Matrix

THE EISENHOWER MATRIX

	URGENT	NOT URGENT
IMPORTANT	DO IT FIRST	SCHEDULE IT
NOT IMPORTANT	DELEGATE IT	DELETE IT

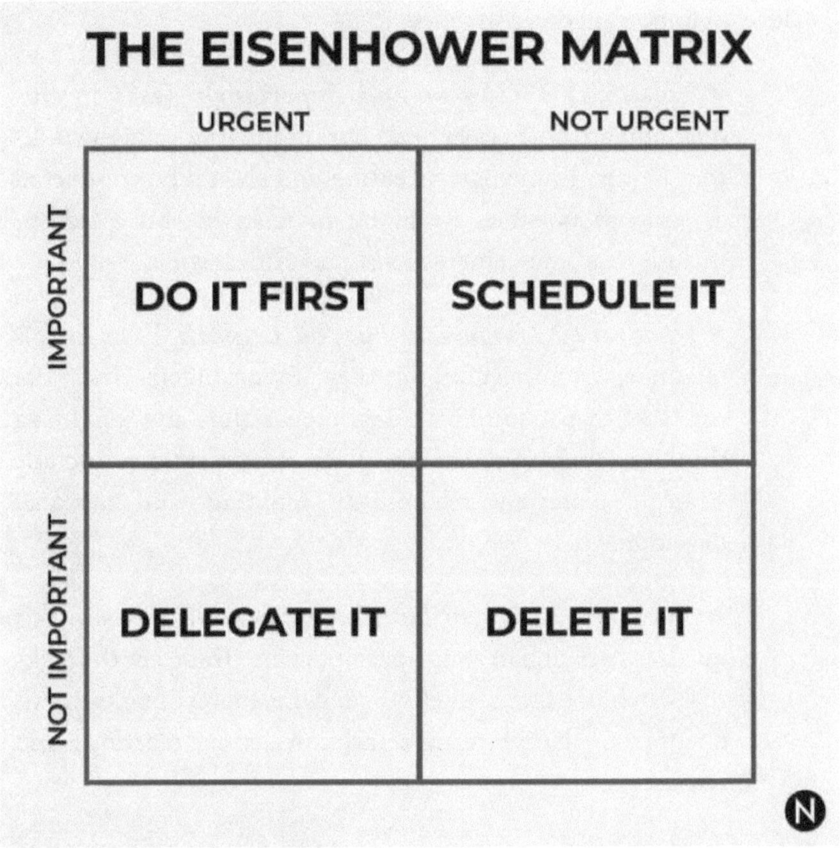

Source: Next Level Gents[1], *The Eisenhower Matrix*[2], December 2023 *(Used with permission)*

------- ◉ -------

What is the Eisenhower Matrix?

---

1.   https://nextlevelgents.com/

2.   *https://nextlevelgents.com/eisenhower-matrix/*

The Eisenhower Matrix *(see Figure 1)* is a four-quadrant grid that helps you classify tasks based on their level of importance and urgency. The matrix is divided into four quadrants, each representing a different level of importance and urgency:

- *Quadrant 1 (Urgent and Important):* Tasks in this quadrant are both urgent *and* important. These are the tasks that require immediate attention and should be completed as soon as possible. Examples of tasks in this quadrant include deadlines, emergencies, and critical issues.

- *Quadrant 2 (Important but Not Urgent):* Tasks in this quadrant are important, but they are not urgent. These are the tasks that require planning, preparation, and long-term thinking. Examples of tasks in this quadrant include strategic planning, relationship building, and personal development.

- *Quadrant 3 (Urgent but Not Important):* Tasks in this quadrant are urgent, but not important. These are the tasks that can be delegated or eliminated. Examples of tasks in this quadrant include interruptions, unnecessary meetings, and emails.

- *Quadrant 4 (Not Urgent and Not Important):* Tasks in this quadrant are neither urgent nor important. These are the tasks that should be eliminated or minimized. Examples of tasks in this quadrant include time-wasting activities, social media, and gossip.

How Does the Eisenhower Matrix Work?

The Eisenhower Matrix works by helping you prioritize tasks based on their level of importance and urgency. By categorizing tasks into one of the four quadrants, you can identify which tasks require immediate attention and which tasks can be delegated, scheduled, or eliminated.

To use the Eisenhower Matrix, follow these six steps:

- *Step 1:* List all of your tasks on a piece of paper or in a digital tool.

- *Step 2:* Categorize each task into one of the four quadrants based on its level of importance and urgency.

- *Step 3:* Prioritize tasks in Quadrant 1 (Urgent and Important) and complete them first.

- *Step 4:* Schedule tasks in Quadrant 2 (Important but Not Urgent) and work on them regularly to ensure they are completed on time.

- *Step 5:* Delegate tasks in Quadrant 3 (Urgent but Not Important) to others if possible, or eliminate them if they are unnecessary.

- *Step 6:* Eliminate tasks in Quadrant 4 (Not Urgent and Not Important) or minimize them to free up more time for important tasks.

Applying the Eisenhower Matrix to Your Career

The Eisenhower Matrix can be a valuable tool in your career, helping you prioritize tasks and become more efficient and productive. Here are five ways you can apply the matrix to your daily routine:

1. ***Prioritize your tasks:*** Use the Eisenhower Matrix to prioritize tasks in your daily to-do list. Focus on completing tasks in Quadrant 1 first and then move on to Quadrant 2.
2. ***Schedule important tasks:*** Use the Eisenhower Matrix to schedule important tasks in Quadrant 2. Set aside time each day or week to work on these tasks and ensure they are completed on time.
3. ***Delegate or eliminate unnecessary tasks:*** Use the Eisenhower Matrix to identify tasks in Quadrant 3 that can be delegated or eliminated. This will help you free up more time for important tasks.
4. ***Minimize time-wasting activities:*** Use the Eisenhower Matrix to identify tasks in Quadrant 4 that are time-wasting activities. Minimize or eliminate these activities to free up more time for important tasks.
5. ***Use the matrix for long-term planning:*** Use the Eisenhower Matrix for long-term planning, such as setting career goals and creating a career development plan. Identify tasks in Quadrant 2 that will help you achieve your goals and schedule time to work on them regularly.

Applying the Eisenhower Matrix to Management

The Eisenhower Matrix can be a very effective tool for management. By categorizing tasks into four quadrants based on their urgency and importance, managers can prioritize their work more effectively and make better decisions about where to allocate their time and resources. This can help managers to be more productive and efficient while also reducing stress and improving job satisfaction. Additionally, by delegating tasks that are not urgent or important, managers can empower their team members and free up their time to focus on more strategic initiatives. Overall, the Eisenhower Matrix is a simple but powerful tool that managers can use to improve their effectiveness and achieve better results.

Conclusion

The Eisenhower Matrix is a simple yet effective tool that can help you prioritize tasks and become more productive and efficient in your career. By categorizing tasks based on their level of importance and urgency, you can identify which tasks require immediate attention and which tasks can be delegated, scheduled, or eliminated. Use the matrix to prioritize your tasks, schedule important tasks, delegate or eliminate unnecessary tasks, minimize time-wasting activities, and plan for the long term. Using the Eisenhower Matrix to your advantage, you can achieve your career goals and become a more successful and productive professional.

Chapter 8
Dickens for Modern Managers
Lessons from "A Tale of Two Cities" for Management Today

Overview

"A Tale of Two Cities" by Charles Dickens is a classic novel that tells the story of the French Revolution. While it may seem like a story about a bygone era, there are actually many lessons that managers today can learn from the book.

This chapter will explore the key themes of "A Tale of Two Cities" and how they can be applied to modern management practices.

1. The Importance of Adaptability

One of the main themes of "A Tale of Two Cities" is the idea of adaptability. Throughout the novel, the characters are forced to adapt to changing circumstances in order to survive. For example, Charles Darnay has to adapt to life in England after leaving behind his aristocratic roots in France. Sydney Carton has to adapt to the fact that he will never be able to be with the woman he loves, and instead finds purpose in sacrificing himself for her and her family.

In the same way, managers need to be adaptable in order to respond to changing circumstances in the workplace. This could involve adapting to changes in technology, changes in the market, or changes in the workforce. Managers who are able to adapt quickly and effectively will be better positioned to succeed in the long run.

2. The Value of Sacrifice

Another key theme of "A Tale of Two Cities" is the idea of sacrifice. The novel is full of characters who make sacrifices for the greater good. Sydney Carton, for example, sacrifices his own life in order to save the life of Charles Darnay and ensure that his family is safe.

In the workplace, managers can learn from this by recognizing the value of sacrifice. This could involve sacrificing short-term gains for long-term success, or sacrificing personal ambitions for the good of the team or company. Managers who are able to lead by example and make sacrifices for the greater good will inspire loyalty and dedication from their employees.

3. The Importance of Communication

Communication is another important theme in "A Tale of Two Cities". Throughout the novel, characters struggle to communicate effectively with one another, often leading to misunderstandings and conflict. For example, Charles Darnay struggles to communicate the truth about his past to his wife and family, leading to tension and mistrust.

In the workplace, effective communication is essential for success. Managers need to be able to communicate clearly and effectively with their employees in order to ensure that everyone is on the same page. This could involve providing regular feedback and updates, listening to employee concerns, and fostering open lines of communication throughout the organization.

4. The Dangers of Complacency

Finally, "A Tale of Two Cities" highlights the dangers of complacency. The novel is set in a time of great social upheaval, and the characters who are complacent or indifferent to the changes around them often suffer the consequences. For example, the Marquis St. Evrémonde is complacent about his position of power and privilege, which ultimately leads to his downfall.

In the workplace, managers need to be aware of the dangers of complacency. It can be easy to become comfortable with the status quo and to resist change, but this can lead to stagnation and decline. Managers willing to embrace change and take risks will be better positioned to succeed in the long run.

Conclusion

In conclusion, "A Tale of Two Cities" is a valuable source of lessons for today's managers. The novel highlights the importance of adaptability, sacrifice, communication, and avoiding complacency. Managers who can apply these lessons in their own work will be well-positioned to succeed in today's fast-paced and ever-changing business environment.

Chapter 9

Identity Management - Using Identified Motivation as a Manager

How to best drive employee engagement and performance

Overview

As a manager, one of your key responsibilities is to motivate and engage your employees. When employees are motivated, they are more productive, committed, and loyal to your organization. However, many managers struggle to find effective ways to motivate their team members and often rely on extrinsic rewards, such as bonuses or promotions, to incentivize performance.

While extrinsic rewards can be effective in the short-term, research shows that they are not sustainable and can even backfire, causing employees to become less motivated over time. Instead, managers should focus on cultivating intrinsic motivation by tapping into what is known as identified motivation.

In this chapter, we will explore what identified motivation is, why it is essential, and how you can use it as a manager to drive employee engagement and performance.

What is Identified Motivation?

Identified motivation is a type of intrinsic motivation that is driven by a clear understanding of the benefits and importance of a specific task or goal. When employees are motivated by identified motivation, they have a strong sense of purpose and believe that what they are doing is valuable and worthwhile.

For example, imagine you are a customer service team manager. If your employees are motivated by identified motivation, they will understand that their work is important because it directly impacts the satisfaction of your customers. They will be motivated to provide excellent customer service not just because it is their job, but because they understand how it contributes to the success of your organization.

Why is Identified Motivation Important?

Identified motivation is important because it is associated with higher levels of engagement, satisfaction, and performance. When employees are motivated by identified motivation, they are more likely to:

- Be committed to their work and your organization
- Be more creative and innovative
- Be more persistent in the face of challenges
- Be more satisfied with their work and their role in the organization
- Have higher levels of well-being and job satisfaction.

In contrast, when employees are motivated primarily by extrinsic rewards, they are more likely to:

- Focus only on the reward and not on the work itself
- Be less committed to the organization and their work
- Take fewer risks and be less innovative

- Be less satisfied with their work and their role in the organization
- Experience higher levels of stress and burnout.

How Can You Use Identified Motivation as a Manager?

Now that we understand what identified motivation is and why it is important, let's explore some practical ways you can use it as a manager to drive employee engagement and performance.

1. Communicate the "why" behind tasks and goals

One of the most important things you can do as a manager is to communicate the "why" behind the tasks and goals you assign to your employees. When employees understand the purpose and importance of their work, they are more likely to be motivated by identified motivation.

For example, let's say that you are assigning a project to a team member. Instead of simply telling them what needs to be done, take the time to explain why the project is important, how it connects to the overall goals of the organization, and how their work will contribute to the success of the project.

2. Provide opportunities for skill development and growth

Employees are more likely to be motivated by identified motivation when they feel that their work is challenging and provides opportunities for growth and development. As a manager, it's important to provide your employees with opportunities to develop new skills, take on new responsibilities, and grow in their roles.

For example, you could offer training programs, mentorship opportunities, or stretch assignments that allow your employees to develop new skills and take on new challenges.

3. Encourage autonomy and decision-making

Employees are more likely to be motivated by identified motivation when they feel that they have autonomy and control over their work. As a manager, it's important to give your employees the freedom to make decisions and take ownership of their work.

For example, instead of micromanaging your employees, give them clear goals and guidelines and then trust them to figure out the best way to achieve those goals. Encourage them to develop new ideas and solutions, and then support them in implementing those ideas.

4. Recognize and celebrate achievements

While intrinsic motivation is driven by a sense of purpose and value, it's still important to recognize and celebrate achievements. As a manager, it's important to acknowledge your employees' hard work and accomplishments and to celebrate their successes.

For example, you could hold regular team meetings where you recognize individual and team achievements, or you could offer small rewards or incentives for exceptional performance.

5. Foster a positive and supportive work environment

Finally, it's important to foster a positive and supportive work environment that encourages intrinsic motivation. As a manager, you can create a positive work environment by:

- Encouraging open communication and feedback
- Providing support and resources to help employees succeed
- Being transparent and honest in your communication
- Encouraging teamwork and collaboration
- Providing opportunities for social connection and camaraderie.

By creating a positive and supportive work environment, you can help your employees feel more motivated and engaged and help them achieve their full potential.

Conclusion

Identified motivation is a powerful tool for managers who want to drive employee engagement and performance. By focusing on cultivating intrinsic motivation, communicating the purpose and value of employees' work, providing opportunities for skill development and growth, encouraging autonomy and decision-making, recognizing and celebrating achievements, and fostering a positive and supportive work environment, you can help your employees feel more motivated, engaged, and committed to your organization.

Chapter 10
The Surprising Commonality to Managing Change and Managing Grief
How to successfully apply the Kübler-Ross Change Management Framework to manage change in your organization

Overview

Change is an inevitable part of life, and this is especially true in management. Managing change effectively can be a challenge no matter what kind of business you are in or the size of your organization. However, having a framework to guide the change process can make it easier. The Kübler-Ross change management framework is one such framework that can be applied to management today.

In this chapter, we will explore how to apply this model to managing any kind of change, which is - by definition - the death of an old way of doing things and the start of a new, post-change future.

The Kübler-Ross Change Management Framework

Elizabeth Kübler-Ross was a Swiss-American psychiatrist and author, born in 1926, who was best known for her work on the stages of grief and the Kübler-Ross model, also known as the five stages of grief. Kübler-Ross was a pioneer in the field of hospice care and palliative medicine and is credited with revolutionizing the way that society views death and dying. She authored many books, including "On Death and Dying," "Death: The Final Stage of Growth," and "Life Lessons." Kübler-Ross passed away in 2004 at the age of 78.

Kübler-Ross' five stages of grief model was originally developed to explain the emotional process of grieving. However, her model can also be applied to change management in business. Hence, it is also commonly referred to as the the Kübler-Ross' change management framework in the area of organizational behavior.

The five stages of grief - and of the Kübler-Ross change management framework - are as follows:

1. Denial
2. Anger
3. Bargaining
4. Depression
5. Acceptance

1. Denial
The first stage of the Kübler-Ross change management framework is denial. In this stage, individuals may refuse to acknowledge that a change is happening or deny that it will have a significant impact. As a manager, it is important to recognize that denial is a normal response to change and to be patient with employees who may be experiencing this stage.

2. Anger
The second stage of the Kübler-Ross change management framework is anger. In this stage, individuals may become frustrated or angry that the change is happening. As a manager, it is important to listen to employees' concerns and address them with empathy.

3. Bargaining
The third stage of the Kübler-Ross change management framework is bargaining. In this stage, individuals may try to negotiate or

compromise in an attempt to avoid the change. As a manager, it is important to be transparent about the reasons for the change and to communicate the benefits clearly.

4. Depression

The fourth stage of the Kübler-Ross change management framework is depression. In this stage, individuals may experience sadness or a sense of loss as they come to terms with the change. As a manager, it is important to provide emotional support and resources to help employees cope with these feelings.

5. Acceptance

The final stage of the Kübler-Ross change management framework is acceptance. In this stage, individuals have come to accept the change and are ready to move forward. As a manager, it is important to celebrate this stage and acknowledge the hard work that employees have put in to get there.

Applying the Kübler-Ross Change Management Framework to Management

To apply the Kübler-Ross change management framework to management, it is important to follow these steps:

1. Identify the change: Identify the specific change that needs to be implemented.

2. Communicate the change: Communicate the change clearly and effectively to all employees.

3. Address concerns: Listen to employees' concerns and address them with empathy.

4. Provide support: Provide emotional support and resources to help employees cope with the change.

5. Celebrate acceptance: Celebrate the final stage of acceptance and acknowledge the hard work that employees have put in to get there.

Applying the Kübler-Ross Change Management Framework to Management Situations

The Kübler-Ross change management framework can be applied to a variety of management situations. Here are some specific examples:

Example 1: Implementing a New Technology System

1. Identify the change: The company is implementing a new technology system to streamline operations.

2. Communicate the change: The company communicates the change to all employees, explaining the benefits of the new system.

3. Address concerns: Employees express concerns about the complexity of the new system and the potential for job loss.

4. Provide support: The company provides training and support to help employees learn the new system and offers reassurance that jobs are not at risk.

5. Celebrate acceptance: As employees become comfortable with the new system, the company celebrates their success and acknowledges their hard work.

Example 2: Restructuring the Organization

1. Identify the change: The company is restructuring the organization to better align with strategic goals.

2. Communicate the change: The company communicates the change to all employees, explaining the reasons for the restructuring and the expected outcomes.

3. Address concerns: Employees express concerns about job security and changes to their roles.

4. Provide support: The company provides counseling and resources to help employees cope with the emotional impact of the restructuring and offers assistance in finding new roles within the organization.

5. Celebrate acceptance: As employees adjust to their new roles and the organization begins to see positive results from the restructuring, the company celebrates their success and acknowledges the hard work of everyone involved.

Example 3: Introducing a New Product Line

1. Identify the change: The company is introducing a new product line to diversify its offerings.

2. Communicate the change: The company communicates the change to all employees, explaining the benefits of the new product line and how it fits into the overall strategy.

3. Address concerns: Employees express concerns about the impact on existing products and the need for additional training.

4. Provide support: The company provides training and support to help employees learn about the new product line and offers reassurance that existing products will not be impacted.

5. Celebrate acceptance: As the new product line gains traction and contributes to the company's success, it celebrates the hard work of employees who contributed to its development and launch.

Conclusion

The Kübler-Ross change management framework can be a useful tool for managing change in a business setting. By following the framework's five stages, managers can help employees navigate the emotional process of change and ultimately come to accept it. By communicating clearly, addressing concerns, providing support, and celebrating acceptance, managers can successfully implement change and help their organization thrive.

Applying the Kübler-Ross change management framework to management situations can help employees navigate the emotional process of change and ultimately come to accept it. By identifying the change, communicating it clearly, addressing concerns, providing support, and celebrating acceptance, managers can successfully implement change and help their organization thrive. These examples demonstrate how the framework can be applied to a variety of management situations, from implementing new technology systems to introducing new product lines.

Chapter 11

Managing Work Transitions with the Bridges' Transition Model

A step-by-step guide for you to use Employing the Bridges' Transition Model to manage organizational change

Overview

The Bridges' Transition Model was developed by William Bridges, a renowned author and consultant. He published his first book on the topic, *"Transitions: Making Sense of Life's Changes,"* in 1980, which delved into the psychological and emotional aspects of transitions. The Bridges' Transition Model was then introduced in his subsequent book, *"Managing Transitions: Making the Most of Change,"* published in 1991. His work was continued on by his wife, Susan, and hence, the model is attributed to both the Bridges.

The Bridges model was initially focused on helping people deal with the personal transitions that come with organizational change. His work gained popularity in the 1980s and 1990s as organizational change became more common and people began to recognize the importance of addressing the psychological and emotional effects of change. Since then, the Bridges' Transition Model has been widely used in various industries and has become a standard framework for managing change.

This chapter provides a look at how the Bridges' Transition Model works and examples of how it can be successfully applied by managers in organizations today.

———◉———

The Bridges' Transition Model

The Bridges' Transition Model is comprised of three stages:

1. Endings
2. The Neutral Zone
3. New Beginnings.

In the *Endings* stage, individuals must acknowledge and grieve the loss of the familiar and comfortable. This time is reserved for saying goodbye to the past and letting go of old habits and ways of thinking.

The *Neutral Zone* is a period of ambiguity and uncertainty that can present challenges as individuals and organizations navigate the unknown and experiment with new approaches.

During the *New Beginnings* stage, individuals and organizations begin to embrace the change and establish new routines and structures. It is a time to focus on the future and move forward with a renewed sense of purpose and direction.

———◉———

Example of Using the Bridges' Transition Model in the Case of a Corporate Acquisition

The Bridges' Transition Model is a useful framework for managing organizational change. It helps leaders and teams navigate the emotional and psychological aspects of transitions, such as layoffs, mergers, and other major changes.

Let's take the example of a company that has just been acquired by a larger organization. The Bridges' Transition Model can be applied in the following way:

1. Endings: The first phase of the model is about acknowledging the endings that come with change. In this case, employees may feel a sense of loss for the company they worked for before the acquisition. Leaders need to communicate transparently and empathetically about the reasons for the acquisition and what it means for the company's future. They should also provide opportunities for employees to express their emotions and concerns.

2. Neutral Zone: The second phase is the neutral zone, where employees are in a state of ambiguity and uncertainty. They may not yet understand the new culture, processes, or expectations of the acquiring company. Leaders can support employees by providing training, coaching, and resources to help them adapt to the changes. They can also encourage employees to collaborate and share their experiences with one another.

3. New Beginnings: The final phase is about creating a new beginning for the organization. Leaders should focus on creating a shared vision and goals for the future of the company. They should involve employees in the planning process and empower them to take ownership of their roles in the new organization. Celebrating milestones and successes along the way can also help build momentum and engagement.

By following the Bridges' Transition Model, leaders can help employees navigate the emotional and psychological aspects of change and create a more successful transition to the new organization.

Example of Applying the Bridges' Transition Model in the Case of Implementing a New Software System

The Bridges' Transition Model is a powerful tool for managing organizational change. Let's consider an example of its application in a company that is transitioning to a new software system.

1. Endings: First, the company is in the endings phase of the transition. Employees are still using the old software system, but they know that the new system is coming, and they are worried about how it will impact their work. The company's leaders recognize that this is a difficult time and take steps to help employees through the transition. They provide training on the new system, hold meetings to discuss concerns, and encourage open communication.

2. Neutral Zone: Next, the company enters the neutral zone. This is a time of uncertainty and confusion as employees try to adapt to the new system. The company continues to offer training and support during this phase. Leaders encourage employees to experiment with the new system and provide feedback on what is working and what is not.

3. New Beginnings: Finally, the company enters the new beginnings phase. Employees have adapted to the new system and are comfortable using it. The company celebrates this achievement and encourages employees to continue to provide feedback to ensure that the new system is meeting their needs.

By using the Bridges' Transition Model, the company was able to manage the change effectively and minimize resistance from employees. The model helped the company's leaders understand the stages of the transition and take appropriate steps to support employees at each stage. As a result, the company was able to successfully implement the new software system with minimal disruption to business operations.

Conclusion

The Bridges' Transition Model underscores the importance of managing the emotional and psychological aspects of change, in addition to practical and logistical factors. It recognizes that change can be difficult, yet with the correct support and mindset, individuals and organizations can successfully navigate through it.

Here's a step-by-step guide for you to use in applying the Bridges' Transition Model to any change that you need to address in an organization as a manager:

1. Identify the Change: The first step in applying the Bridges' Transition Model is to identify the change that needs to be managed. This could be a merger or acquisition, a change in leadership, a new technology implementation, or any other major change.

2. Communicate the Change: Once the change has been identified, it is important to communicate it to all those who will be affected. This includes employees, stakeholders, and customers. Communication should be clear, transparent, and empathetic, and should address any concerns and questions that people may have.

3. Endings: The first phase of the Bridges' Transition Model is about acknowledging the endings that come with change. This involves helping people to let go of the past and move forward. This could involve saying goodbye to old habits, processes, or ways of thinking.

4. Neutral Zone: The second phase is the "neutral zone," where individuals and organizations are in a state of ambiguity and uncertainty. This is a period of experimentation and exploration, where new ways of doing things are tried out and tested. It is important to provide support and resources during this phase to help people adapt to the changes.

5. New Beginnings: The final phase is about creating a new beginning for the organization. This involves establishing new routines, processes, and structures. It is important to involve people in this phase and to empower them to take ownership of their roles in the new organization.

6. *Celebrate Success:* Finally, it is important to celebrate success and milestones along the way. This helps to build momentum and engagement and keeps people motivated and committed to the change process.

Chapter 12

The ADKAR Change Management Model - A Comprehensive Overview

How do you lead change - and make it stick? The ADKAR model is a proven way to make change work that you need to know about - and use!

Overview

Change is a constant in all aspects of life, and organizations are no exception. As organizations strive to remain competitive, they must continuously adapt to new technologies, processes, and strategies. However, change can be difficult to implement, and the failure rate of organizational change initiatives is alarmingly high. According to a study by McKinsey & Company, only 30% of organizational change initiatives succeed, while the remaining 70% fail or fall short of their objectives. The ADKAR change management model is a framework developed to help organizations manage change effectively and increase the likelihood of successful adoption.

The ADKAR model focuses on the individual and the steps they must go through to embrace and implement change. The model emphasizes that individuals must go through a series of stages to be successful in making a change. Each stage builds on the previous one, and if any stage is missed or not fully addressed, the change initiative is likely to fail.

This chapter will provide a comprehensive overview of the ADKAR change management model, including its history, components, and strengths and limitations. It will then examine its applications and provide the reader with an example of an ADKAR-focused change effort in an organization.

Historical Background

The ADKAR change management model was developed by Jeffrey Hiatt, the founder of Prosci, a leading provider of change management tools and training programs. Hiatt developed the model in the late 1990s as a response to the high failure rate of change initiatives. He recognized that traditional change management models focused primarily on the organizational aspects of change, such as processes, systems, and structures, and neglected the individual and their role in change. Hiatt's goal was to create a model that would help organizations understand the human side of change and provide a roadmap for managing change at the individual level.

Components of the ADKAR Model

The ADKAR model is based on five components, which together form a roadmap for successful change management. These components form the acronym, "ADKAR," and are:

1. *A*wareness (of the need for change).
2. *D*esire (to participate in and support the change).
3. *K*nowledge (of how to change).
4. *A*bility (to change).
5. *R*einforcement (to sustain the change)

Each component represents a stage that individuals must go through to embrace and implement change successfully.

1. Awareness

The first stage of the ADKAR model is *Awareness*. This stage involves creating an understanding of the need for change and why it is necessary. The Awareness stage is critical because it sets the foundation for the entire change initiative. If individuals are not aware of the need for change, they are unlikely to support it fully. Awareness can be created through communication, training, and education.

2. Desire

The second stage of the ADKAR model is **Desire**. The Desire stage involves creating a desire or motivation to support the change. The Desire stage is critical because it ensures that individuals are committed to the change and willing to invest the time and effort required to make it happen. Desire can be created by highlighting the benefits of the change and how it will improve the individual's work or the organization's performance.

3. Knowledge

The third stage of the ADKAR model is **Knowledge**. The Knowledge stage involves providing individuals with the skills and information they need to make the change successfully. The Knowledge stage is critical because it ensures that individuals are equipped to implement the change effectively. Knowledge can be provided through training, coaching, and mentoring.

4. Ability

The fourth stage of the ADKAR model is *Ability*. The Ability stage involves providing individuals with the resources and support they need to implement the change. The Ability stage is critical because it ensures that individuals have the capability to implement the change successfully. Ability can be provided through resources such as technology, tools, and processes, as well as ongoing support and feedback.

5. Reinforcement

The fifth and final stage of the ADKAR model is *Reinforcement*. The Reinforcement stage involves recognizing and rewarding individuals for their efforts and successes in implementing the change. The Reinforcement stage is critical because it ensures that individuals are motivated to continue to support the change and are recognized for their contributions. Reinforcement can be provided through recognition programs, incentives, and ongoing feedback.

Strengths and Limitations of the ADKAR Model

The ADKAR model has several strengths that make it an effective change management framework. These strengths include its focus on the individual, its structured approach, and its flexibility. The model's focus on the individual ensures that change initiatives take into account the human side of change, which is often overlooked in traditional change management models. The structured approach of the model ensures that each stage of the change process is addressed, minimizing the risk of failure. The model's flexibility allows it to be applied to a wide range of change initiatives, making it a versatile framework.

However, the ADKAR model also has some limitations. One limitation is that it can be time-consuming and resource-intensive to implement fully. The model requires a significant investment of time and resources to ensure that each stage is addressed adequately. Another limitation is that the model's focus on the individual may neglect the organizational aspects of change. While the model recognizes the importance of the organizational context, it may not provide sufficient guidance on how to manage the organizational aspects of change effectively.

Applications of the ADKAR Model

The ADKAR model has a broad range of applications and can be used in various contexts, including organizational change, project management, and personal development.

Organizational Change

The ADKAR model is widely used in organizational change management. It provides a roadmap for managing change at the individual level and ensures that individuals are fully engaged and committed to the change initiative. The model can be used to manage a wide range of organizational changes, such as new technology implementations, process improvements, and organizational restructuring.

Project Management

The ADKAR model can also be used in project management. It provides a framework for managing change within a specific project and ensures that individuals are equipped to implement the change successfully. The model can be used to manage a range of projects, such as new product launches, process improvements, and system implementations.

Personal Development

The ADKAR model can also be used in personal development. It provides a roadmap for individuals to make personal changes successfully. The model can be used to manage personal changes such as adopting a healthier lifestyle, learning a new skill, or changing a behavior.

Application of the ADKAR Change Management Model to Organizational Change

Organizations are continuously evolving, and change is a critical component of this evolution. However, implementing change in an organization can be challenging, and the failure rate of organizational change initiatives is high. The ADKAR change management model provides a framework for managing change effectively at the individual level. This model can be applied to organizational change to ensure that individuals are fully engaged and committed to the change initiative. In this section, we will provide an example of how the ADKAR change management model can be applied to organizational change.

———●———

Example: Implementing a New Performance Management System

Suppose an organization decides to implement a new performance management system. The organization recognizes that the current system is outdated and does not align with the organization's goals and objectives. The organization also recognizes that implementing a new system may be challenging, and employees may be resistant to change. To manage this change effectively, the organization decides to use the ADKAR change management model.

Awareness

At this first stage *(ADKAR)*, the organization creates an understanding of the need for change and why it is necessary. The organization communicates the need for the new performance management system to employees and explains how it aligns with the organization's goals and objectives. The organization also communicates how the new system will benefit employees by providing more accurate performance feedback and facilitating career development.

Desire

In this second stage *(ADKAR)*, the organization creates a desire or motivation to support the change. The organization highlights the benefits of the new performance management system and how it will improve the employee's work experience. The organization also provides opportunities for employees to provide feedback and contribute to the design of the new system, creating a sense of ownership and commitment to the change.

Knowledge

In this third stage *(ADKAR)*, the organization provides employees with the skills and information they need to make the change successfully. The organization provides training on the new performance management system, including how to use it, how it aligns with the organization's goals and objectives, and how it will benefit employees. The organization also provides coaching and mentoring to ensure that employees feel confident in their ability to use the new system effectively.

Ability

In this fourth stage *(ADKAR)*, the organization provides employees with the resources and support they need to implement the change. The organization provides access to technology, tools, and processes needed to use the new performance management system effectively. The organization also provides ongoing support and feedback, ensuring that employees have the capability to implement and use the new system successfully.

Reinforcement

In this fifth and final stage *(ADKAR)*, the organization recognizes and rewards employees for their efforts and successes in implementing the change. The organization provides recognition and incentives to employees who use the new performance management system effectively, reinforcing the change's importance and motivating employees to continue to support it.

Analysis

In the example provided above, the ADKAR change management model was used to implement a new performance management system. The model's structured approach ensured that each stage of the change process was addressed, minimizing the risk of failure. By using the ADKAR change management model, the organization was able to successfully implement the new performance management system and improve the employee's work experience.

Conclusion

The ADKAR change management model is a comprehensive framework that provides a roadmap for managing change effectively. The model's focus on the individual and its structured approach ensures that each stage of the change process is addressed, minimizing the risk of failure. The model's flexibility allows it to be applied to a wide range of change initiatives, making it a versatile framework. This model can be applied to organizational change to ensure that individuals are fully engaged and committed to the change initiative. While the model has some limitations, its strengths make it an effective framework for managing change in organizations, projects, and personal development.

Chapter 13
Why and How Skunkworks Work
If you are managing a project, here's why this trusted method may be the best way to drive innovation and success.

Overview

In today's fast-paced business environment, project teams often struggle to keep up with their stakeholders' demands. Whether it's a new product launch, software application development, or marketing campaign, the pressure to deliver results quickly can be intense. In such situations, Skunkworks can be an ideal solution to meet the team's needs.

What is a Skunkwork?

A Skunkwork is a team or project group that is given a high degree of autonomy and freedom to explore, experiment, and develop new ideas without the constraints of the usual organizational bureaucracy. The term "Skunkworks" was first coined by Lockheed Martin in the 1940s to describe a small, isolated group of engineers who were tasked with developing a new aircraft. The team was located in a small, unmarked building on the outskirts of the company's facility, and they were given the freedom to work on the project without any interference from the rest of the organization. The name "Skunkworks" was inspired by the comic strip "Li'l Abner", which featured a secret moonshine operation called "Skonk Works."

The Skunkworks team responsible for developing the new aircraft was led by Clarence "Kelly" Johnson, a brilliant engineer who had previously worked on some of Lockheed Martin's most successful projects. Johnson believed that the traditional bureaucratic approach to engineering was too slow and cumbersome and that a small, focused team of engineers could develop new technologies and products much more quickly and efficiently.

Under Johnson's leadership, the Skunkworks team developed a number of groundbreaking aircraft, including the U-2 spy plane, the SR-71 Blackbird, and the F-117 stealth fighter. These aircraft were developed in record time and pushed the boundaries of what was possible in aerospace engineering.

The success of the Skunkworks approach at Lockheed Martin inspired other companies to adopt similar methods for developing new products and technologies. Skunkworks became a popular approach for companies looking to break free from the constraints of traditional organizational bureaucracy and foster innovation and creativity.

Skunkworks Today

Today, Skunkworks can be found across a wide range of industries, from technology and software development to marketing and advertising. They are typically small, focused teams that are given a high degree of autonomy and freedom to explore new ideas and develop new products or technologies without the constraints of traditional organizational bureaucracy.

The legacy of the Skunkworks approach can be seen in some of the most innovative and successful companies in the world, from Google and Apple to SpaceX and Tesla. By fostering a culture of innovation, creativity, and agility, Skunkworks have helped these companies stay ahead of the curve and drive growth and success for years to come.

Why a Skunkworks May Be Ideal for Your Project Team

Today, Skunkworks have become a popular approach for companies looking to develop new products, services, or technologies quickly and efficiently. Here are some reasons why a Skunkwork may be the ideal answer for your project team:

1. Autonomy and Freedom

One of the key benefits of a Skunkwork is the autonomy and freedom it provides to the team members. In a traditional organizational setting, teams are often constrained by rules, regulations, and bureaucracy, which can slow down the innovation process. With a Skunkwork, team members are given the freedom to take risks, experiment, and explore new ideas without the fear of failure. This can lead to more creativity and innovation and, ultimately, better results.

2. Speed and Efficiency

Skunkworks are designed to be fast and efficient. The team is usually small and focused, with a clear mandate and a sense of urgency. This allows them to work quickly and make decisions rapidly without getting bogged down in meetings, approvals, and other bureaucratic processes. This speed and efficiency can be critical in today's fast-changing business environment, where the ability to respond quickly to market trends and customer needs is essential.

3. Flexibility and Agility

Skunkworks are also highly flexible and agile. They are designed to adapt quickly to changing circumstances and to pivot if necessary. This is important in today's business environment, where the pace of change is rapid and unpredictable. Skunkworks can help companies stay ahead of the curve by enabling them to respond quickly to market shifts and customer demands.

4. Innovation and Creativity

Skunkworks are designed to foster innovation and creativity. They provide team members with the freedom to think creatively and to come up with new ideas without fear of criticism or rejection. This can lead to breakthrough innovations that can transform an organization or an industry. Skunkworks can also help companies stay ahead of the competition by developing new products, services, or technologies that set them apart from their rivals.

5. Motivation and Engagement

Finally, Skunkworks can be highly motivating and engaging for team members. They provide a sense of purpose and a feeling of empowerment that can be lacking in traditional organizational settings. This can lead to higher levels of engagement, productivity, and job satisfaction, which can ultimately benefit the entire organization.

How to Implement a Skunkworks

If you're considering a Skunkworks for your project team, be sure to carefully consider your goals, your team's capabilities, and the resources you'll need to make it a success. With the right approach, a Skunkworks can be a powerful tool for driving innovation and growth in your organization. However, creating a successful Skunkworks requires careful planning, execution, and ongoing management. In this section of the chapter, we'll explore the steps involved in implementing a Skunkworks and provide some tips for making it a success.

Step 1: Define Your Goals and Objectives

The first step in implementing a Skunkworks is to define your goals and objectives. What do you hope to achieve with your Skunkworks? Are you looking to develop a new product, service, or technology? Are you trying to improve an existing process or system? Are you looking to explore new markets or customer segments? Clearly defining your goals and objectives will help you determine the scope of your Skunkworks and ensure that everyone involved is aligned on the objectives.

Step 2: Identify Your Team

The next step is to identify the team that will be responsible for your Skunkworks. This team should be small, focused, and highly motivated. Ideally, they should have a mix of skills and expertise that are relevant to your goals and objectives. You may need to look beyond your existing workforce to find the right people for your Skunkworks. Consider recruiting from outside your organization or partnering with a startup or academic institution to bring in fresh talent and ideas.

Step 3: Allocate Resources

Once you've identified your team, it's time to allocate the resources they'll need to be successful. This may include funding, equipment, software, and other resources. Make sure your Skunkworks team has everything they need to be productive and efficient. You may need to work with your finance department to secure additional funding or resources, so be sure to clearly communicate the value of your Skunkworks and the expected ROI.

Step 4: Establish Autonomy and Freedom

One of the key characteristics of a Skunkworks is autonomy and freedom. Your Skunkworks team should be given the freedom to explore, experiment, and innovate without the constraints of traditional organizational bureaucracy. This means giving them the authority to make decisions, take risks, and pivot if necessary. You may need to create a separate physical space for your Skunkworks team to work, away from the rest of the organization, to ensure they have the freedom they need to be successful.

Step 5: Set Clear Expectations and Metrics

While autonomy and freedom are important, it's also essential to set clear expectations and metrics for your Skunkworks team. This will help ensure that they stay focused on the goals and objectives of the Skunkworks and that their efforts are aligned with the needs of the organization. Set clear milestones, deadlines, and deliverables, and regularly review progress to ensure that your team is on track.

Step 6: Foster Collaboration and Communication

Despite the autonomy and freedom that a Skunkwork provides, it's also important to foster collaboration and communication among your team members. Encourage them to share ideas, insights, and feedback with each other, and create opportunities for them to collaborate with other teams or departments within your organization. Regular check-ins and status updates can help keep everyone on the same page and ensure that your Skunkworks is integrated with the rest of your organization.

Step 7: Celebrate Success and Learn from Failure

Finally, it's important to celebrate your Skunkworks team's successes and learn from their failures. Make sure to recognize their achievements and share them with the rest of the organization so that everyone can appreciate the value of your Skunkwork effort. At the same time, be prepared for the possibility of failure. Not every Skunkworks will be successful, but every failure can be a valuable learning experience that can inform future efforts.

⎯⎯⎯⎯◉⎯⎯⎯⎯

Conclusion

As we have seen, the Skunkwork idea has a remarkable past and has been applied successfully by leading companies today. As such, Skunkworks can be an ideal solution for project teams looking to innovate, create, and deliver results quickly and efficiently. They provide autonomy, speed, flexibility, innovation, and motivation, all of which can help teams achieve their goals and exceed their stakeholders' expectations.

Implementing a Skunkwork can be a powerful tool for driving innovation, creativity, and agility in your organization. By following these steps and best practices, you can create a Skunkworks that is aligned with your goals and objectives and delivers measurable results. Remember to stay flexible and adaptable and to adjust your approach as needed based on feedback and results. With the right approach, a Skunkwork can help your organization stay ahead of the curve and drive growth and success for years to come.

Chapter 14
Working through the 8 Steps of the Kotter Change Management Model

How to Increase the Odds of Successful Change in Today's Organizations

Overview

Change is an inevitable part of any organization, and managing change effectively is critical to the success of any business. In today's fast-paced and ever-changing business landscape, organizations need to be agile and adaptable to stay ahead of the competition. However, managing change can be a daunting task, and many organizations struggle with it. That's where the Kotter change management model comes in. Developed by Dr. John Kotter, a renowned change management expert and an emeritus professor at Harvard Business School, this model provides a structured approach to managing change and helps organizations navigate the complexities of change.

The Kotter change management model consists of eight steps that can be used to guide an organization through the change management process. In this chapter, we will explore each step and provide examples of how they can be applied in practice.

Step 1: Establish a Sense of Urgency

The first step in the Kotter change management model is to establish a sense of urgency. This involves creating a compelling reason for change and communicating it effectively to the organization. The goal is to create a sense of urgency that motivates people to take action and embrace change.

For example, let's say XYZ Corporation is struggling with declining sales and is in danger of losing market share. The CEO can establish a sense of urgency by communicating the risks associated with this decline and the need for change to address the issue.

Step 2: Form a Powerful Coalition

The second step in the Kotter change management model is to form a powerful coalition. This involves bringing together a group of influential people who can support the change effort and drive it forward. These individuals should have the necessary skills, resources, and authority to make things happen.

For example, in the case of XYZ Corporation, the CEO can form a coalition of senior executives, department heads, and key stakeholders who can work together to drive the change effort forward.

Step 3: Create a Vision for Change

The third step in the Kotter change management model is to create a vision for change. This involves developing a clear and compelling vision of what the future will look like after the change has been implemented. The vision should be inspiring, ambitious, and align with the organization's values and goals.

For example, the CEO of XYZ Corporation can create a vision for change that involves transforming the company into a leader in the industry and achieving sustainable growth through innovation and customer-centricity.

———◆———

Step 4: Communicate the Vision

The fourth step in the Kotter change management model is to communicate the vision. This involves communicating the vision in a way that resonates with the organization and inspires people to take action. The goal is to ensure that everyone understands the vision and is committed to it.

For example, the CEO of XYZ Corporation can communicate the vision through town hall meetings, emails, newsletters, and other communication channels. The key is to ensure that the message is consistent, clear, and compelling.

———◆———

Step 5: Empower Others to Act on the Vision

The fifth step in the Kotter change management model is to empower others to act on the vision. This involves removing any obstacles that may prevent people from taking action and providing the necessary resources and support to enable them to act on the vision.

For example, the CEO of XYZ Corporation can empower employees by providing training, resources, and support to help them embrace the change and take ownership of the vision.

———◆———

Step 6: Create Short-Term Wins

The sixth step in the Kotter change management model is to create short-term wins. This involves celebrating small successes along the way to keep people motivated and engaged. The goal is to build momentum and demonstrate that the change effort is making progress.

For example, XYZ Corporation can create short-term wins by launching a new product or service that addresses a customer pain point or by achieving a revenue target.

Step 7: Consolidate Gains and Produce More Change

The seventh step in the Kotter change management model is to consolidate gains and produce more change. This involves building on the momentum created by the short-term wins and continuing to drive the change effort forward. The goal is to embed the change into the organization's culture and ensure its sustainability.

For example, XYZ Corporation can consolidate gains by establishing new processes and systems that support the change effort and by continuing to innovate and improve.

Step 8: Anchor New Approaches in the Organization's Culture

The final step in the Kotter change management model is to anchor new approaches in the organization's culture. This involves embedding the change into the organization's DNA and ensuring that it becomes part of the way things are done. The goal is to make the change a permanent part of the organization and to ensure its sustainability.

For example, XYZ Corporation can anchor new approaches in its culture by aligning its values and culture with the vision for change and by ensuring that the change is reflected in all aspects of the organization's operations.

Conclusion

The Kotter change management model provides a structured approach to managing change and can help organizations navigate the complexities of change. By following the eight steps outlined above and applying them in practice, organizations can increase their chances of success in managing change and achieving their goals.

Chapter 15
The Inventive and Productive Team - How to Best Manage a Team of Creatives
A how-to-guide for managing creative teams

Overview

Managing a team of creatives can be a challenging proposition. Creatives are often driven by their passions and their desire for artistic expression. Creatives are also fiercely independent. This can make them difficult to manage. However, with the right approach, managing creatives can be a rewarding experience that leads to great results. In this chapter, we'll explore some of the main challenges you may face when managing creatives and provide tips on how to best manage creative teams.

Challenges in Managing Creative Teams

1. Balancing Artistic Freedom with Business Goals

One of the biggest challenges when managing creatives is balancing artistic freedom with business goals. Creatives are often driven by a desire to express themselves, which can sometimes conflict with the need to produce work that meets business objectives. As a manager, it's your job to find a balance between these two competing priorities.

To achieve this balance, you may need to spend time discussing your business goals with your team and helping them understand how their work fits into the larger picture. You may also need to provide guidance and feedback to ensure that their work meets business objectives without sacrificing creativity.

2. Managing Different Personalities

Another challenge when managing creatives is managing different personalities. Creatives are often passionate and opinionated, which can lead to conflicts and disagreements within the team. As a manager, it's your job to manage these personalities and ensure that everyone is working together effectively.

To manage different personalities, you may need to spend time getting to know your team members and understanding what motivates them. You may also need to be a mediator when conflicts arise and provide guidance on how to resolve disagreements in a constructive way.

3. Managing Creative Blocks

Creatives can sometimes experience creative blocks, which can be frustrating for both the individual and the team. As a manager, it's your job to help your team members overcome these blocks and continue producing high-quality work.

To manage creative blocks, you may need to provide your team with the resources they need to succeed, such as access to new tools and technology or training in new techniques. You may also need to provide guidance and support to help them overcome their blocks and stay motivated.

4. Managing Time and Budget Constraints

Finally, managing time and budget constraints can be a challenge when managing creatives. Creatives can sometimes get carried away with their work, leading to missed deadlines and budget overruns. As a manager, it's your job to ensure that your team is working within the constraints of time and budget.

To manage time and budget constraints, you may need to set clear expectations from the outset and monitor progress regularly. You may also need to provide guidance and support to help your team stay on track and ensure that their work meets quality standards within the constraints of time and budget.

Tips for Managing Creative Teams

By understanding the challenges you may face when managing creatives and adopting strategies to overcome them, you can manage your team effectively and produce great results. Here are some practical tips for managing creative teams:

1. Understand Your Team

First and foremost, it's essential to understand your team of creatives. Creatives are often motivated by different things than other team members. They may be driven by a desire for artistic expression, a need to innovate, or a desire to make a real impact on the world. As a manager, it's your job to understand what motivates each member of your team and tailor your management style to suit their needs.

One way to understand your team is to have regular one-on-one meetings with each member. During these meetings, you can discuss their goals, aspirations, and concerns. You can also provide feedback on their work and offer guidance on how they can improve. By taking the time to get to know your team members, you'll be better equipped to manage them effectively.

2. Foster a Creative Culture

To get the most out of your creative team, it's important to foster a creative culture within your organization. This means creating an environment where creativity is encouraged and innovation is rewarded. You can do this by providing your team with the resources they need to be successful, such as access to the latest tools and technology.

You should also encourage your team to share their ideas and collaborate with one another. This can be achieved by holding brainstorming sessions, team-building exercises, and other activities that promote collaboration and creativity. By fostering a creative culture, you will be able to motivate your team and inspire them to produce their best work.

3. Set Clear Expectations

Setting clear expectations is essential when managing creatives. Creatives are often driven by a desire to express themselves and be creative, which can lead to ambiguity around what is expected of them. As a manager, it's your job to set clear expectations around deadlines, budgets, and quality standards.

You should also be clear about what success looks like and how it will be measured. This will help your team understand what they need to do to achieve their goals and will give them a sense of direction. By setting clear expectations, you'll be able to manage your team more effectively and ensure that everyone is on the same page.

4. Provide Feedback

Providing feedback is crucial when managing creatives. Creatives are often passionate about their work, and they need feedback to know how they're doing. However, it's important to provide feedback in a way that is constructive and supportive.

When providing feedback, start with positives, then move on to areas where improvement is needed. Be specific about what needs to be improved, and provide suggestions on how the person can improve. Also, be sure to listen to your team's feedback and incorporate it into your management style. By providing feedback, you'll be able to help your team grow and improve.

5. Empower Your Team

Empowering your team is an important part of managing creatives. Creatives are often motivated by a sense of ownership over their work, so it's important to give them the autonomy they need to be successful.

This means delegating tasks and giving your team the freedom to make decisions.

You should also encourage your team to take risks and try new things. This can be scary, but it's essential for creativity and innovation. By empowering your team, you'll be able to create a culture that values creativity and innovation.

———◈———

Conclusion

Managing creatives can be a challenging task, but it's also incredibly rewarding. By understanding your team, fostering a creative culture, setting clear expectations, providing feedback, and empowering your team, you'll be able to manage your team effectively and produce great results.

Chapter 16

The "Secret Sauce" - Keeping Corporate Culture Strong with Remote Workers

Companies with a large percentage of their workforce working remotely face great challenges in building and maintaining a strong culture. Here's how to do it today.

Overview

With the rise of remote work, many companies are struggling to maintain their corporate culture. A strong corporate culture can help keep employees engaged, motivated, and productive. But when employees are working from different locations, it can be challenging to keep everyone on the same page.

In this chapter, we will discuss some tactics companies can use to keep their corporate culture strong with remote workers and look at firms that have done so successfully.

Keeping Your Corporate Culture Strong in a Remote Environment

1. Define Your Corporate Culture

The first step in keeping your corporate culture strong with remote workers is to define your culture. What are the values, beliefs, and behaviors that your company stands for? What makes your company unique?

Once you have defined your corporate culture, make sure everyone on your team understands it. This can be done through onboarding materials, regular communication, and training sessions.

2. Communicate Regularly

Communication is key when it comes to maintaining a strong corporate culture. With remote workers, it's important to have regular check-ins to keep everyone on the same page. This can be done through video conferencing, instant messaging, or email.

It's also essential to create a culture of transparency. Be open and honest with your team about what's going on in the company. Share updates on company goals, achievements, and challenges.

3. Foster a Sense of Community

One of the biggest challenges with remote work is the lack of social interaction. To combat this, companies should try to foster a sense of community among their remote workers.

This can be done through virtual team-building activities, online forums, and social events. Encourage your team to get to know each other and build relationships.

4. Provide the Right Tools

Remote workers need the right tools to be productive and engaged. Make sure your team has access to the technology they need to do their jobs effectively. This includes communication tools, project management software, and collaboration platforms.

5. Recognize and Reward Success

Finally, it's important to recognize and reward success. Remote workers can sometimes feel disconnected from the company, so it's important to show them that their contributions are valued.

This can be done through regular feedback, bonuses, and recognition programs. Celebrate milestones and achievements, and make sure your team knows that their hard work is appreciated.

<hr>

Companies That Have Winning Remote Cultures

There are several companies that have successfully maintained a strong corporate culture with remote workers. Here are but a few examples:

1. GitLab

GitLab is a software development company with over 1,300 employees working remotely. The company has a strong culture of transparency and communication, with regular virtual team-building events and an open-door policy. They also have a comprehensive onboarding process for new remote workers and encourage employees to share feedback and ideas.

2. InVision

InVision is a digital product design platform with a fully remote workforce. The company has a strong focus on employee engagement, with regular virtual coffee breaks, team-building activities, and a company-wide chat channel. They also have a dedicated team that provides support and resources for remote workers.

3. Zapier

Zapier is a web automation tool with a remote team of over 300 employees. The company has a strong culture of trust and autonomy, with flexible work hours and a results-oriented approach. They also have a comprehensive onboarding process and a remote work playbook that outlines best practices and guidelines for remote workers.

4. Buffer

Buffer is a social media management company with a fully remote team. The company has a strong culture of transparency and feedback, with regular one-on-one meetings and a company-wide feedback process. They also have a focus on employee wellness, with a dedicated team that provides resources and support for remote workers.

5. Automattic

Automattic is the company behind WordPress.com and has a fully remote workforce of over 1,100 employees. The company has a strong culture of flexibility and autonomy, with no set work hours or schedules. They also have a dedicated team that provides support and resources for remote workers, including a travel stipend and a home office setup allowance.

The "Secret Sauce"

So, what is the "secret sauce" that these companies have used to build a strong remote work culture? They have been successful in maintaining a strong corporate culture with remote workers by prioritizing communication, community, and employee engagement. They have also put in place processes and resources to support remote workers and ensure that they feel connected to the company and its values.

Conclusion

Maintaining a strong corporate culture with remote workers can be challenging, but as these companies have shown, it's not impossible. By defining your culture, communicating regularly, fostering a sense of community, providing the right tools, and recognizing success, you can keep your team engaged, motivated, and productive.

Remember, a strong corporate culture is essential for *any* company's success. With the right strategies in place, you can maintain that culture even with remote workers.

Chapter 17

Porter's Five Forces - Do They Still "Work" in Today's Business Environment?

The Five Forces Model is a bedrock of business strategy thinking. But with rapid technological, social, and economic change, is it still accurate in describing competitive environments?

Overview

The Five Forces Model is an analytical tool used to evaluate the competitive environment of a particular industry. The model was first proposed by Michael E. Porter, a renowned Harvard Business School professor, in 1979, and it has since become a widely used framework for analyzing the competitive forces that shape industries and markets. The model is based on the idea that the level of competition in an industry is determined by five key factors, which are:

1. Bargaining power of suppliers
2. Bargaining power of buyers
3. Threat of new entrants
4. Threat of substitute products or services
5. The intensity of competitive rivalry.

The framework suggests that the intensity of these forces determines the level of competition in the industry and, consequently, the profitability of the companies operating in it.

In this chapter, we will provide a comprehensive overview of Porter's Five Forces Model, explaining each of the five forces in detail, and discussing how the model can be used to analyze the competitive environment of different industries. However, with the rapid technological advancements and the changing dynamics of the business environment, it is natural to question whether the Porter's Five Forces framework still applies today. We will thus explore this question and analyze the relevance of Porter's Five Forces in today's business environment.

The Five Forces Framework

Bargaining Power of Suppliers

The bargaining power of suppliers is the first force that Porter's Five Forces Model considers. This force refers to the degree to which suppliers can influence the price and quality of the goods or services they provide to a particular industry. Suppliers can exert significant bargaining power if they are the sole source of a critical input or if they have a strong brand reputation.

For example, if a particular industry relies heavily on a specific raw material that is only available from a limited number of suppliers, those suppliers will have a strong bargaining position. In such a case, the suppliers can demand higher prices for their inputs, which can increase the cost of production for the industry and decrease its profitability.

Bargaining Power of Buyers

The bargaining power of buyers is the second force that Porter's Five Forces Model considers. This force refers to the degree to which buyers can influence the price and quality of the goods or services they purchase from a particular industry. Buyers can exert significant bargaining power if they purchase large volumes of a product or service, if they have a lot of alternative options to choose from, or if they are highly informed about the industry and its products.

For example, if a particular industry produces a product that is highly commoditized and has many substitutes, buyers will have a strong bargaining position. In such a case, buyers can demand lower prices and higher quality products, which can decrease the profitability of the industry.

Threat of New Entrants

The threat of new entrants is the third force that Porter's Five Forces Model considers. This force refers to the degree to which new competitors can enter a particular industry and compete with existing firms. The threat of new entrants can be influenced by factors such as the cost of entry, the level of brand recognition required to succeed, and the regulatory environment.

For example, if a particular industry has high barriers to entry, such as significant capital requirements or complex regulatory requirements, new entrants will face significant challenges when trying to enter the market. However, if the industry is relatively easy to enter and there are few barriers to entry, new competitors are more likely to enter the market and increase competition.

Threat of Substitute Products or Services

The threat of substitute products or services is the fourth force that Porter's Five Forces Model considers. This force refers to the degree to which consumers can switch to alternative products or services that serve the same purpose as those offered by a particular industry. The threat of substitute products or services can be influenced by factors such as the availability and affordability of substitutes, the level of product differentiation, and the switching costs for consumers.

For example, if a particular industry produces a product that is easily replaceable by a cheaper or more convenient substitute, such as a generic medication that can replace a name-brand medication, the industry will face significant competition from the substitutes. However, if the industry produces a highly differentiated product that is difficult to substitute, such as a luxury car, the threat of substitute products will be relatively low.

Intensity of Competitive Rivalry

The intensity of competitive rivalry is the fifth and final force that Porter's Five Forces Model considers. This force refers to the degree to which existing firms in a particular industry compete with each other. The intensity of competitive rivalry can be influenced by factors such as the number of competitors in the market, the level of marketing and advertising spending, and the degree of product differentiation.

For example, if a particular industry has many competitors that produce similar products or services, the intensity of competitive rivalry will be high. In such a case, firms will compete aggressively on price, quality, and marketing, which can decrease the profitability of the industry.

Applicability of Porter's Framework Today

So, does the Porter Five Forces Model still "work" today? In this section of the chapter, we will explore each of the five forces in the context of the current business and technological environment.

Bargaining Power of Suppliers

The bargaining power of suppliers refers to the ability of suppliers to influence the price and quality of the products or services they provide. In today's business environment, the globalization of supply chains and the emergence of alternative suppliers have reduced the bargaining power of suppliers. Companies can now source products and services from different regions and suppliers, which has increased competition among suppliers and reduced their bargaining power. Additionally, the use of technology has enabled companies to streamline their procurement processes and negotiate better deals with suppliers. Therefore, it can be argued that the bargaining power of suppliers is less relevant today than it was in the past.

Bargaining Power of Buyers

The bargaining power of buyers relates to the ability of customers to influence the price and quality of the products or services they purchase. In today's business environment, the availability of information and the emergence of online platforms have significantly increased the bargaining power of buyers. Customers can now compare prices and quality of products from different suppliers and make informed purchasing decisions. Additionally, the use of social media platforms has enabled customers to share their experiences and influence the purchasing decisions of others. Therefore, it can be argued that the bargaining power of buyers is more relevant today than it was in the past and businesses must focus on providing high-quality products and services to meet customer demands.

Threat of New Entrants

The threat of new entrants relates to the ease with which new competitors can enter the industry. In today's business environment, the barriers to entry have significantly reduced due to rapid technological advancements and the availability of resources. The emergence of e-commerce platforms and the sharing economy has enabled new entrants to access a wider customer base and compete with established players in the industry. For instance, Uber, a ride-hailing company, disrupted the traditional taxi industry by leveraging technology to offer a seamless and convenient service. Therefore, it can be argued that the threat of new entrants still applies today, and businesses must constantly innovate and improve their offerings to stay relevant.

Threat of Substitute Products or Services

The threat of substitute products or services refers to the availability of alternative products or services that can satisfy customer needs. In today's business environment, the emergence of technology and the sharing economy has enabled customers to access a wide range of substitute products and services. For instance, the emergence of online streaming services has disrupted the traditional cable TV industry. Therefore, it can be argued that the threat of substitute products or services still applies today, and businesses must constantly innovate to stay ahead of the competition.

Intensity of Competitive Rivalry

The rivalry among existing competitors relates to the intensity of competition among the players in the industry. In today's business environment, the emergence of technology and the globalization of markets have significantly increased the intensity of competition. Companies can now operate globally and compete with players from different regions. Additionally, the emergence of e-commerce platforms has enabled small businesses to compete with established players in the industry. Therefore, it can be argued that the rivalry among existing competitors is more relevant today than it was in the past, and businesses must constantly innovate and improve their offerings to stay ahead of the competition.

Conclusion

The Five Forces Model is a powerful analytical tool that can help businesses and investors understand the competitive environment of different industries. By considering each of the five forces, businesses can identify the key drivers of competition in their industry and develop strategies to gain - or protect - a competitive advantage. However, it is important to note that the model is not a one-size-fits-all solution and that each industry is unique and must be analyzed on its own merits.

It can be argued that Porter's Five Forces framework still applies today, although the relevance of each force has changed due to rapid technological advancements and the changing dynamics of the business environment. Therefore, businesses must constantly adapt and innovate to stay ahead of the competition and gain a competitive advantage in their industry.

Chapter 18

The Sports Book Fallacy

Why great sports coaches may actually not be the best role models for leading and managing in the workplace

Overview

One of the great traditions in sports is that once a coach wins a championship - or has any degree of success, many of them choose to write books on how what they do in their sport applies more generally. Indeed, there have been several coaches over the years who have written best-selling business books. Here are a just a few examples:

1. Phil Jackson

Phil Jackson is a retired NBA coach who won 11 championships as a coach, and two as a player. In *"Sacred Hoops,"* he shared the leadership strategies and philosophy that helped him build a winning team culture.

2. John Wooden

John Wooden was one of the most successful coaches in the history of college basketball. Over the course of his coaching career, he amassed an impressive record of 664 wins and just 162 losses, for a winning percentage of .804. He coached at UCLA from 1948 to 1975, leading the Bruins to 10 NCAA championships, including seven in a row from 1967 to 1973. Wooden was known for his attention to detail, his emphasis on fundamentals, and his ability to motivate his players to perform at their best. He was also known for his commitment to teaching life lessons through sports, and his Pyramid of Success remains a popular model for personal development and leadership. In *"Wooden on Leadership,"* he shares his principles of leadership, including the importance of character, integrity, and hard work.

3. Tony Dungy

Tony Dungy is a former NFL coach who won a Super Bowl with the Indianapolis Colts. In *"Quiet Strength,"* he shares his philosophy of leadership, which emphasizes the importance of faith, family, and service.

4. Bill Walsh

Bill Walsh was a legendary NFL coach who won three Super Bowls with the San Francisco 49ers. In *"The Score Takes Care of Itself,"* he shares his leadership principles, which include a focus on preparation, attention to detail, and a commitment to excellence.

These coaches have applied their leadership skills in the sports world and have written books sharing their insights, which have proven to be valuable in the business world as well.

Yes, sports coaches are often looked up to as role models for their ability to lead and inspire their teams to victory. However, when it comes to management in the workplace, sports coaches may not always be the best role models for managers. In this chapter, we'll explore why this is the case in terms of:

- The differences in the environments of sports and business
- The differences in the relationship between the leader and their charges
- The differences in individual versus collective success
- The differences in motivational tactics, and
- The differences in the skill set needed to succeed.

The Differences in the Environments of Sports and Business

Firstly, sports coaches operate in a very different environment than managers in the workplace. In sports, the objective is to win at all costs. This means that coaches often employ aggressive tactics to get the results they want. While this may work in the short term, it's not a sustainable approach to management in the workplace.

In the workplace, the goal is not just to achieve short-term success but to build a team that can work together effectively over the long term. This requires a different approach to management, one that emphasizes collaboration, communication, and respect for each individual's unique skills and contributions.

The Differences in the Relationship between the Leader and Their Charges

Additionally, sports coaches often have a very different relationship with their players than managers have with their employees. In sports, the coach is often seen as a figure of authority who must be obeyed without question. Players are expected to follow the coach's instructions, no matter how harsh or demanding they may be.

In the workplace, however, managers must collaborate with their employees to achieve their goals. It's important for managers to listen to their employees' ideas and concerns and work together to find solutions to problems. This requires a much more collaborative approach than the authoritarian style often employed by sports coaches.

The Differences in Individual Versus Collective Success

Another reason why sports coaches are not good role models for managers is that they often prioritize winning over all else. This can lead to a culture of cutthroat competition, where employees are pitted against one another in a race to achieve individual success at the expense of the team's overall success.

In the workplace, however, managers must prioritize the success of the team as a whole. This means fostering a culture of collaboration and teamwork, where employees work together to achieve shared goals and support one another in their individual roles.

The Differences in Motivational Tactics

Additionally, sports coaches often use fear and intimidation as motivational tactics. They may yell at players, criticize them harshly in public, or threaten to bench them if they don't perform up to the coach's standards. While this may motivate some players to work harder in the short term, it's not a sustainable approach to motivation in the workplace.

In the workplace, managers must motivate their employees in a more positive and constructive way. This means providing regular feedback, recognizing individual accomplishments, and creating a culture of support and encouragement.

The Differences in the Skill Set Needed to Succeed

Finally, sports coaches often have a very different skill set than managers in the workplace. While sports coaches may be experts in strategy and tactics on the field, they may not have the necessary skills to manage people effectively in the workplace. This can lead to a lack of understanding of the unique challenges faced by employees in the workplace and an inability to manage and motivate them effectively.

Conclusion

While sports coaches may be successful leaders in their own right, they are not necessarily good role models for managers in other industries. The focus on short-term success, hierarchical leadership style, and individual achievement that are often emphasized in sports coaching can be counterproductive in a business setting. Instead, managers should focus on fostering a collaborative and inclusive culture, prioritizing long-term sustainability, and balancing the needs of their team with the needs of the company as a whole. By doing so, they can create a positive work environment where their team can thrive and succeed over the long term.

Chapter 19
The Next Best Thing to Being There
Successfully Employing Substitutes for Leadership Theory in Management Today

Overview

Substitutes for leadership theory is a leadership theory that focuses on situational factors that can substitute for or neutralize the impact of a leader's actions. The theory suggests that there are certain factors that can replace the need for a leader to exert influence over their followers. These factors include things like task structure, group cohesion, individual skills and experience, and formalization of procedures.

The theory's basic premise is that in certain situations, leaders are not necessary to motivate and direct their followers. Instead, the situational factors are strong enough to provide the necessary motivation and direction. In these situations, the leader's actions have little or no effect on the outcome of the group's performance.

In this chapter, we will explore the concept of substitutes for leadership theory in more detail, including its history, key concepts, and examples of how it has been applied in real-world situations. We then look specifically at how substitutes for leadership theory can - and are - being used successfully to manage remote workers today.

Origins of Substitutes for Leadership Theory

Substitutes for leadership theory was first proposed by Steven Kerr and John Jermier in their 1978 article "Substitutes for Leadership: Their Meaning and Measurement." The article was published in Organizational Behavior and Human Performance. At the time, Kerr and Jermier were both professors of organizational behavior at the University of Southern California at the time. They were interested in exploring the idea that in some situations, leaders were not necessary to motivate and direct their followers. They believed that there were certain situational factors that could substitute for or neutralize the impact of a leader's actions.

The theory was developed in response to the growing interest in contingency theories of leadership, which suggested that the effectiveness of a leader depended on the situation they were in. Substitutes for leadership theory takes this idea a step further by suggesting that in some situations, leaders are completely unnecessary.

The article was well-received in the academic community and quickly became one of the most cited articles in the field of organizational behavior. It led to a number of follow-up studies and further development of the theory.

Key Concepts of Substitutes for Leadership Theory

There are several key concepts that are central to substitutes for leadership theory. These concepts include:

1. Substitutes

Substitutes are situational factors that can replace or neutralize the impact of a leader's actions. These factors can be internal or external to the organization.

Internal substitutes include things like task structure, group cohesion, individual skills and experience, and formalization of procedures. External substitutes include things like market competition, government regulations, and technological advancements.

2. Neutralizers

Neutralizers are situational factors that cancel out or reduce the impact of a leader's actions. These factors can be internal or external to the organization.

Internal neutralizers include things like ambiguity, role conflict, and low task interdependence. External neutralizers include things like economic conditions, political instability, and social unrest.

3. Enhancers

Enhancers are situational factors that amplify or increase the impact of a leader's actions. These factors can be internal or external to the organization.

Internal enhancers include things like high task interdependence, role clarity, and high group cohesion. External enhancers include things like strong market demand, favorable economic conditions, and political stability.

4. Leadership Styles

Leadership styles are the behaviors and actions of a leader that affect their ability to motivate and direct their followers. There are many different leadership styles, including transformational, transactional, autocratic, democratic, and laissez-faire.

Examples of Substitutes for Leadership Theory

Substitutes for leadership theory has been applied in a number of real-world situations over the years. Here are but a few examples:

1. Military Operations

Substitutes for leadership theory has been applied in military operations, where the chain of command and formalized procedures can substitute for the need for a leader to exert influence over their followers. In highly structured and formalized military operations, everyone knows exactly what is expected of them, and there is little room for individual decision-making. In these situations, the leader's role is simply to ensure that everyone follows the established procedures.

2. Self-Managing Teams

Substitutes for leadership theory has also been applied in self-managing teams, where the team members are responsible for their own motivation and direction. In these teams, the members are typically highly skilled and experienced, and they are able to work together effectively without the need for a leader to guide them. The team members are typically given a great deal of autonomy and are trusted to make decisions on their own.

3. Professional Sports Teams

Substitutes for leadership theory has also been applied in professional sports teams, where the team's performance is determined by the skills and experience of the individual players. In these teams, the coach's role is to provide guidance and direction, but the players are responsible for their own motivation and performance. The coach's influence is limited, and the team's success is determined largely by the individual players' abilities.

Substitutes for Leadership Theory in Today's Remote Work Environment

In today's increasingly remote work environment, there are some substitutes for leadership theory that can be effective. For example, self-leadership can be a powerful tool for employees who are working from home. This means that individuals take ownership of their own work and motivation and don't necessarily need a leader to motivate them.

Another substitute for leadership in remote work is a focus on clear communication and expectations. When everyone is working remotely, clear communication is essential to keep everyone on the same page. This means that leaders need to be clear about their expectations and communicate them effectively to their team.

Additionally, technology can be used as a substitute for leadership in remote work environments. Project management tools, virtual meeting software, and other digital tools can help employees stay organized and connected, even when they're working remotely.

Overall, these substitutes for leadership can be effective in a remote work environment, as long as they are implemented properly and with clear communication.

Companies That Have Successfully Implemented Substitutes for Leadership in Remote Work

Substitutes for leadership theory suggests that in certain situations, leadership is not necessary. In the context of remote work, this theory suggests that there are certain factors that can substitute for leadership and enable employees to work effectively without constant oversight from their managers. Some examples of companies using substitutes for leadership in remote work include Netflix, GitHub, and InVision.

1. Netflix

Netflix, for instance, offers its employees unlimited vacation time and encourages them to take ownership of their work. This means that employees are trusted to manage their own time and responsibilities, without the need for constant supervision from their managers.

2. GitHub

GitHub, a software development company, operates on the principle of "working openly." This means that employees are encouraged to collaborate and share their work with others, which creates a sense of accountability and responsibility among team members. As a result, employees are empowered to work independently and take ownership of their projects.

3. InVision

InVision, a design and prototyping tool, has a remote team that operates on a results-only work environment (ROWE). This means that employees are evaluated based on the results they deliver, rather than the number of hours they work. This approach allows employees to work on their own terms and take ownership of their work, without the need for constant supervision or micromanagement.

Overall, these companies demonstrate that substituting leadership with trust, accountability, and ownership can lead to effective remote work and high employee satisfaction.

Conclusion

Substitutes for leadership theory is a leadership theory that focuses on situational factors that can substitute for or neutralize the impact of a leader's actions. The theory suggests that in certain situations, leaders are not necessary to motivate and direct their followers. Instead, the situational factors are strong enough to provide the necessary motivation and direction.

Substitutes for leadership theory has been applied in a number of real-world situations, including military operations, self-managing teams, and professional sports teams. In these situations, the situational factors are strong enough to provide the necessary motivation and direction, and the leader's role is limited. As we have seen, substitutes for leadership can also work effectively in remote work environments to help workers better manage their own work and "fit" into the organization wherever they may be.

Chapter 20
The Minimum Viable Product (MVP) Strategy
The proven wisdom of launching your product or service with a minimal version to learn how to best construct and market it for the long run

Overview

The *Minimum Viable Product (MVP)* is a product development strategy that has taken the startup world by storm. It is a concept that involves creating a basic version of a product with just enough features to satisfy early adopters and gather feedback for future development. The goal is to launch the product quickly and inexpensively, test the market, and learn what customers want and need. By releasing an MVP, startups can validate their assumptions, minimize the risk of failure, and iterate based on real-world feedback.

The MVP concept has become particularly popular in the tech industry and is widely used by startups and established companies alike. In this chapter, we will look at the MVP concept in more detail, its benefits, how to create an MVP, and some examples of successful MVPs.

What is an MVP?

An MVP is a product that has the minimum set of features required to satisfy early customers and gather feedback for future development. It is not a prototype or a beta version but a real product that is launched in the market. The idea behind an MVP is to test the market as soon as possible and to learn from customer feedback. By doing so, startups can validate their assumptions, minimize the risk of failure, and iterate based on real-world feedback.

The MVP concept was popularized by Eric Ries in his book *"The Lean Startup."* According to Ries, an MVP is "the version of a new product which allows a team to collect the maximum amount of validated learning about customers with the least effort." He goes on to say that "the goal of an MVP is to test fundamental business hypotheses and to help entrepreneurs begin the learning process as quickly as possible."

Benefits of an MVP

The MVP concept has several benefits for startups and established companies alike. Here are some of them:

1. Validate Assumptions: Startups often have many assumptions about their customers, product, and market. By releasing an MVP, startups can test these assumptions and validate them with real-world feedback.

2. Minimize Risk: Launching a full-fledged product without testing the market can be risky and expensive. By launching an MVP, startups can minimize the risk of failure and reduce costs.

3. Learn from Customer Feedback: Startups can learn what customers want and need by gathering feedback from early adopters. This feedback can be used to improve the product and make it more attractive to a wider audience.

4. Iterate Based on Feedback: Startups can use the feedback gathered from an MVP to iterate and improve the product. By doing so, they can create a product that meets the needs of their customers and is more likely to succeed in the market.

5. Faster Time to Market: By launching an MVP, startups can get their product to market faster and start generating revenue sooner.

Creating an MVP

Creating an MVP requires careful planning and execution. Here are some steps that startups can follow to create an MVP:

1. Identify the Problem: Start by identifying a specific problem that your product solves. This problem should be significant enough to motivate customers to use your product.

2. Define the Value Proposition: Define the value proposition of your product. This is a statement that explains how your product solves the problem and why customers should use it.

3. Identify the Minimum Set of Features: Identify the minimum set of features required to solve the problem and provide value to customers. These features should be the core of your product and should be easy to use and understand.

4. Build the MVP: Build the MVP using the minimum set of features. The MVP should be a real product that is launched in the market.

5. Test the Market: Launch the MVP in the market and gather feedback from early adopters. Use this feedback to improve the product and iterate.

Examples of Successful MVPs

Here are some examples of successful MVPs:

1. *Dropbox:* Dropbox launched in 2008 with an MVP that had just enough features to store and share files. The MVP was so successful that it generated 75,000 signups in its first week.

2. *Airbnb:* Airbnb launched in 2008 with an MVP that allowed people to rent out air mattresses in their living rooms. The MVP was successful and led to the creation of a multi-billion dollar company.

3. *Instagram:* Instagram launched in 2010 with an MVP that allowed people to share photos with filters. The MVP was successful and led to the creation of a social media giant that was eventually acquired by Facebook.

Other examples of a Minimum Viable Product include a basic mobile app with core functionality, a landing page with a sign-up form for a new service, a prototype of a physical product with a limited set of features, or a simple version of a software program with only the essential features needed to solve a specific problem. The key is to create a product with just enough features to satisfy early adopters and collect feedback for future iterations.

Conclusion

The Minimum Viable Product (MVP) is a product development strategy that has become popular in the tech industry. It involves creating a basic version of a product with just enough features to satisfy early adopters and gather feedback for future development. By releasing an MVP, startups can validate their assumptions, minimize the risk of failure, and iterate based on real-world feedback. The MVP concept has several benefits, including validating assumptions, minimizing risk, learning from customer feedback, iterating based on feedback, and faster time to market. Creating an MVP requires careful planning and execution, and successful examples include Dropbox, Airbnb, and Instagram.

Chapter 21
The CRAAP Test

How management can - and should - use this framework to ensure it is managing based on reliable information, not, well, crap!

Overview

In today's information age, it is essential to have access to reliable and accurate information. This is particularly important in the business world, where decisions are made on a daily basis that can have a significant impact on an organization's success. However, with so much information available, it can be challenging to determine what is reliable and what is not. This is where the CRAAP Test comes in. In this chapter, we will discuss how management can use the CRAAP Test to ensure reliable information.

What is the CRAAP Test?

The CRAAP Test is a set of criteria used to evaluate information sources based on their reliability and credibility. CRAAP stands for Currency, Relevance, Authority, Accuracy, and Purpose. Students, researchers, and librarians often use the test to determine whether a source is appropriate for use in academic or professional settings. By applying the CRAAP Test, one can assess the quality of information and make informed decisions about its use.

Let us take a look at each of these criteria in detail.

Currency: This criterion refers to the timeliness of the information. It is essential to consider when the information was published or last updated. Outdated information may not be relevant or accurate.

Relevance: This criterion refers to how well the information relates to your research topic or question. The information should be directly related to your needs and should provide useful insights.

Authority: This criterion refers to the source of the information. It is essential to consider the author's credentials, the publisher, and the reputation of the source. The information should come from a reputable source.

Accuracy: This criterion refers to the reliability and truthfulness of the information. It is essential to ensure that the information is supported by evidence and facts.

Purpose: This criterion refers to the reason why the information was created. It is essential to consider whether the information is biased or objective and whether there is any underlying agenda.

Why is the CRAAP Test Important for Management?

In today's fast-paced business environment, managers need to make informed decisions quickly. They need to have access to reliable and accurate information to make the right choices. The CRAAP Test can help managers ensure that the information they are using is reliable and accurate. By using the CRAAP Test, managers can:

1. Avoid Using Outdated Information: The Currency criterion of the CRAAP Test can help managers identify outdated information.

This is particularly important in fields where the information changes rapidly, such as technology and healthcare.

2. Ensure Relevance: The Relevance criterion of the CRAAP Test can help managers ensure that the information they are using is directly related to their research topic or question. This can save time and ensure that managers are not wasting their efforts on irrelevant information.

3. Verify Authority: The Authority criterion of the CRAAP Test can help managers ensure that the information they are using comes from a reputable source. This can help managers avoid using information that is biased or has an underlying agenda.

4. Verify Accuracy: The Accuracy criterion of the CRAAP Test can help managers ensure that the information they are using is reliable and truthful. This can help managers avoid making decisions based on false or incorrect information.

5. Identify Bias: The Purpose criterion of the CRAAP Test can help managers identify bias in the information they are using. This can help managers avoid making decisions based on information that is biased or has an underlying agenda.

How to Use the CRAAP Test in Management

Now that we have discussed the CRAAP Test's importance for management, let's examine how managers can use it to ensure reliable information.

1. Determine Your Information Needs: The first step in using the CRAAP Test is to determine your information needs. What information do you need, and why do you need it? This will help you identify the relevance and purpose of the information.

2. Identify Potential Sources: The next step is to identify potential sources of information. This can include books, articles, websites, and reports. When selecting potential sources, consider the authority of the source and its reputation.

3. Apply the CRAAP Test: Once you have identified potential sources, apply the CRAAP Test to each source. Consider the Currency, Relevance, Authority, Accuracy, and Purpose of the information. This will help you identify reliable sources of information.

4. Verify the Information: Once you have identified reliable sources of information, verify the information. This can include checking the facts and evidence presented in the information.

5. Use the Information: Once you have verified the information, you can use it to make informed decisions. This can include making business decisions, developing strategies, or conducting research.

Conclusion

The CRAAP Test is a powerful tool that can help managers ensure reliable and accurate information. By using the CRAAP Test, managers can avoid using outdated or biased information and make informed decisions quickly. The CRAAP Test is easy to use and can be applied to a wide range of information sources. Managers who use the CRAAP Test can be confident that they are using reliable and accurate information to make the right decisions.

Chapter 22

Idea Sex: No, It's Not What You Think, It's Better!

How management can use this provocative method to develop better and more creative business strategies

Overview

The concept of "idea sex" has become increasingly popular in recent years, as businesses and organizations seek new and innovative ways to set their strategy. Idea sex involves combining two or more seemingly unrelated ideas to create a new and innovative concept. This approach can be particularly useful for management teams looking to set their business strategy, as it allows them to draw upon a wide range of ideas and perspectives from different fields and disciplines.

In this chapter, we will explore what idea sex is and how management can use idea sex to set their business strategy, and the benefits that this approach can provide.

What is "Idea Sex?"

Before we dive into how management can use idea sex, let's first define what it is. The term "idea sex" was coined by James Altucher, an American entrepreneur and author. It refers to the process of combining two or more seemingly unrelated ideas to create a new and innovative concept.

The basic idea is that when two ideas are combined, their offspring can be more powerful and valuable than either of the parents. For example, the combination of GPS technology and social media has given rise to location-based marketing, a new and effective way to reach customers based on their physical location.

Idea sex is a way to generate fresh and creative ideas by cross-pollinating different fields and disciplines. The concept encourages people to think outside the box and to connect disparate ideas in new and interesting ways.

Benefits of Implementing Idea Sex

1. Encouraging Diverse Perspectives

One of the key benefits of using idea sex to set business strategy is that it encourages diverse perspectives. By combining ideas from different fields and disciplines, management can draw upon a wider range of experiences and viewpoints, which can lead to more creative and innovative solutions.

For example, if a management team is looking to set a strategy for a new product launch, they might bring together individuals from different departments, such as marketing, engineering, and customer support. Each of these individuals will bring their own unique perspective and expertise to the table, which can help to identify potential challenges and opportunities that might otherwise have been overlooked.

2. Fostering Creativity and Innovation

Another benefit of using idea sex to set business strategy is that it fosters creativity and innovation. By combining seemingly unrelated ideas, management can generate new and innovative concepts that might not have been possible otherwise.

For example, Apple's iPod was not the first portable music player on the market. However, by combining the idea of a portable music player with the idea of a digital music store, Apple was able to create a product that revolutionized the music industry. This approach not only led to increased revenue for Apple, but it also changed the way that people consume music today.

3. Identifying New Opportunities

By drawing upon a wide range of ideas and perspectives, management can also identify new opportunities that might not have been obvious before. This can be particularly useful in industries that are undergoing significant change, such as technology or healthcare.

For example, in the healthcare industry, the combination of data analytics and wearable technology has led to the development of remote patient monitoring systems. These systems allow healthcare providers to monitor patients' vital signs and health status remotely, which can lead to more efficient and effective care.

4. Enhancing Decision Making

Using idea sex to set business strategy can also enhance decision making. By drawing upon a wide range of ideas and perspectives, management can make more informed decisions that are based on a broad range of data and insights.

For example, if a management team is considering a new product launch, they might use idea sex to gather input from different departments and stakeholders. This can help to identify potential challenges and opportunities, as well as to assess the feasibility of the project.

5. Improving Communication and Collaboration

Finally, using idea sex to set business strategy can improve communication and collaboration within an organization. By bringing together individuals from different departments and backgrounds, management can foster a culture of collaboration and innovation that can lead to improved outcomes.

For example, if a management team is working on a new project, they might use idea sex to encourage collaboration and communication between different departments. This can help to ensure that everyone is working towards the same goal and that the project is completed on time and within budget.

Implementing Idea Sex in Business Strategy

Now that we've established the benefits of using idea sex for business strategy, let's explore how management can implement it. Here are some practical tips:

1. Encourage cross-functional collaboration

One of the keys to successful idea sex is collaboration across different functions and departments. Managers should encourage employees from different departments to work together and share their ideas. For example, marketing and engineering teams can work together to develop new products that meet customer needs.

2. Embrace diversity

Diversity of thought and perspective is essential for idea sex to be effective. Managers should embrace diversity in their teams and encourage employees to bring their unique perspectives to the table. This can lead to new and innovative ideas that would not have been possible with a homogeneous team.

3. Provide resources and support

Implementing idea sex requires time, resources, and support from management. Managers should allocate resources and provide support to teams that are working on new and innovative ideas. This can include funding for research and development, access to technology and equipment, and training and development programs.

4. Foster a culture of experimentation

Idea sex requires experimentation and risk-taking. Managers should foster a culture of experimentation where employees are encouraged to try new things, even if they are not guaranteed to succeed. This can lead to breakthrough ideas that can transform the business.

5. Continuously evaluate and iterate

Finally, idea sex is an iterative process. Managers should continuously evaluate and iterate on their ideas to refine and improve them. This can involve testing new products or services with customers, collecting feedback, and making adjustments based on that feedback.

Conclusion

Idea sex can be a powerful tool for management teams looking to set their business strategy. By encouraging diverse perspectives, fostering creativity and innovation, identifying new opportunities, enhancing decision-making, and improving communication and collaboration, this approach can help to drive business success and growth.

In today's fast-paced and ever-changing business environment, companies need to be innovative and adaptable to stay ahead of the competition. Idea sex is a powerful tool that managers can use to generate new and creative ideas for their business strategy. By encouraging cross-functional collaboration, embracing diversity, providing resources and support, fostering a culture of experimentation, and continuously evaluating and iterating, companies can use idea sex to identify new and untapped markets, stay ahead of the competition, and adapt to changing market conditions.

Chapter 23

Managing Knowledge in an Age of Employee Free Agency

A realistic how-to-guide for knowledge management today

Overview

Employee turnover is a major challenge that companies face today. When employees leave, they take with them valuable knowledge and expertise that can be difficult to replace. However, companies can mitigate the impact of turnover by employing knowledge management strategies that enable them to capture and retain critical knowledge.

Turnover Today

With the increasing demand for skilled labor and the rise of the gig economy, employees have more options than ever before when it comes to their employment. As a result, companies must work harder to retain their employees and minimize turnover. Here are some of the key factors driving employee turnover in today's job market:

1. Competitive job market

The current job market is highly competitive, with many companies vying for the same pool of skilled workers. As a result, employees have more options than ever before and may be more likely to leave their current employer in search of better opportunities.

2. Lack of job satisfaction

Employees today are looking for more than just a steady paycheck. They want to feel engaged and fulfilled in their work, and if they don't feel that way, they may be more likely to leave their current position.

3. Limited opportunities for advancement

Employees want to know that they have opportunities for growth and advancement within their organization. If they feel that there are limited opportunities for advancement, they may be more likely to look for opportunities elsewhere.

4. Poor work-life balance

With the rise of technology and the ability to work remotely, employees are increasingly looking for employers that offer a good work-life balance. If they feel that their current employer is not supportive of their work-life balance, they may be more likely to look for opportunities elsewhere.

5. Inadequate compensation

Employees today are more aware of their market value and are less likely to stay with an employer that does not offer competitive compensation packages.

Knowledge Management

When an employee walks out the door, all too often, the knowledge and expertise that he or she possesses walks out the door with them. Here are some ways that companies can use knowledge management to address the challenge of turnover:

1. Develop a knowledge transfer strategy

When employees leave, it is important to ensure that their knowledge is transferred to their replacements or to other team members. This can be achieved by developing a formal knowledge transfer strategy that identifies the key knowledge areas that need to be transferred and the most effective methods for doing so.

2. Implement a knowledge management system

A knowledge management system can help companies capture and store critical knowledge in a centralized repository. This can include documents, reports, and other types of content that are relevant to the organization. By making this information easily accessible, companies can ensure that it is not lost when employees leave.

3. Encourage knowledge sharing

Knowledge sharing is a key component of knowledge management. Encouraging employees to share their knowledge and expertise can help ensure that it is not lost when they leave the company. This can be achieved by creating a culture of knowledge sharing and providing opportunities for employees to share their knowledge with others.

4. Provide training and development opportunities

Providing training and development opportunities for employees can help ensure that they are equipped with the knowledge and skills they need to perform their jobs effectively. This can also help to retain employees by providing them with opportunities for growth and development.

5. Conduct exit interviews

When employees leave, it is important to conduct exit interviews to capture their feedback and insights. This can help identify areas where the company can improve and enable the company to capture any knowledge that the employee may have that is relevant to the organization.

6. Leverage technology

Technology can play an important role in knowledge management. Tools such as collaboration platforms, social media, and knowledge management software can facilitate the sharing of knowledge and make it easier to capture and store critical information.

Conclusion

Employee turnover is a challenge that companies face today, but by employing knowledge management strategies, companies can mitigate the impact of turnover. By developing a knowledge transfer strategy, implementing a knowledge management system, encouraging knowledge sharing, providing training and development opportunities, conducting exit interviews, and leveraging technology, companies can capture and retain critical knowledge and ensure that it is not lost when employees leave. By doing so, companies can remain innovative, agile, and responsive to changes in the job market, and continue to thrive in a highly competitive business environment.

Chapter 24

"You Might Want to Be Sitting Down for This One"

A how-to guide for delivering the bad news as a manager

Overview

Delivering bad news as a manager is a difficult task that requires tact, empathy, and clear communication. Whether it is letting an employee know they didn't receive a promotion or informing a team that the company is going through tough times, delivering bad news is never easy. However, there are ways to do it effectively and with compassion. In this chapter, we will discuss some tips on how to deliver bad news as a manager.

1. Prepare Yourself

Before you deliver any bad news, it is important to prepare yourself. Make sure you have all the facts straight and that you understand the situation fully. It's also important to think about how you will communicate the news. Will you do it in person or over the phone? Will you have a private meeting, or will you announce it to the whole team? These are all important considerations that will impact how the news is received.

2. Be Honest and Direct

When delivering bad news, it's important to be honest and direct. Don't sugarcoat the news or try to minimize the impact. Instead, be clear and concise about what is happening and what the consequences are. This will help ensure that everyone is on the same page and that there are no misunderstandings.

3. Show Empathy

Showing empathy is essential when delivering bad news. Put yourself in the other person's shoes and try to understand how they are feeling. Acknowledge their emotions and validate their concerns. This will help them feel heard and respected, even if the news is difficult to hear.

4. Offer Support

After delivering bad news, it's important to offer support. This could include providing resources to help the person or team cope with the news, or offering to help in any way you can. Let them know that you are there for them and that you will do everything you can to support them through this difficult time.

5. Follow Up

It's important to follow up after delivering bad news. Check in with the person or team to see how they are doing and if there's anything you can do to help. This will show that you care and that you're committed to helping them through the situation.

6. Focus on the Future

While bad news can be difficult to hear, it's important to focus on the future. Help the person or team see that there are still opportunities for growth and development, even in the face of adversity. This will help them stay motivated and focused on their goals.

7. Learn from the Experience

Finally, it's important to learn from the experience. Take some time to reflect on how you delivered the news and what you could have done differently. Use this as an opportunity to grow and improve your communication skills so you can deliver bad news more effectively in the future.

Conclusion

Delivering bad news well is important for a manager for several reasons. Firstly, it helps to maintain trust and credibility with employees or team members. When a manager is transparent and honest about bad news, it shows that they respect and value their employees enough to share the truth with them. Secondly, delivering bad news well can help to minimize uncertainty and anxiety in the workplace. By providing clear and concise information about the situation, employees can feel more informed and prepared to deal with the consequences. Lastly, a manager who delivers bad news well shows that they are empathetic and care about the well-being of their employees. This can help to boost morale and create a positive work culture, even in difficult times.

And while delivering bad news as a manager is never easy, but it can be done effectively with the right approach. By preparing yourself, being honest and direct, showing empathy, offering support, following up, focusing on the future, and learning from the experience, you can deliver bad news with compassion and professionalism.

Chapter 25
Managing with a Lottery Mentality
The dangers of managing by chance and how to avoid this management trap

Overview

As a manager, it can be tempting to take risks and make decisions based on chance. This is the "lottery mentality" - a management approach where decisions are made based on chance rather than sound reasoning or analysis

But relying on a lottery mentality can have serious consequences for you as a manager, your team, and, yes, your entire company. The lottery mentality can manifest in a number of ways in the workplace. For example, a manager might:

1. Hire a candidate based on a gut feeling or personal connection rather than conducting a thorough evaluation of their skills and experience.

2. Make a major investment without fully understanding the potential risks and rewards or without conducting a proper analysis of the market or industry.

3. Allocate resources based on who seems to need them most rather than who has the most pressing needs or the best potential for success.

4. Make decisions based on personal biases or hidden agendas rather than taking a more objective and rational approach.

5. Rely on luck or chance to determine outcomes rather than developing a clear strategy or plan of action based on data and analysis.

While these decisions may sometimes work out in the short term, they can ultimately lead to inconsistent results, a lack of accountability, a lack of trust, and a lack of innovation and focus in the workplace.

The Dangers of Managing with a Lottery Mentality

Here are just a few of the dangers of managing with a lottery mentality:

1. You may miss out on top talent.

When you rely on your instincts to make hiring decisions, you may overlook candidates who are truly qualified and well-suited for the job. This can lead to a less skilled and less productive team, which can ultimately harm your bottom line.

2. Your investments may not pay off.

Making investments without fully understanding the potential risks and rewards can be a recipe for disaster. You may end up sinking resources into a project that ultimately fails, leaving you with nothing to show for your efforts.

3. You may create a toxic workplace culture.

If you allocate resources based on who seems to need them most, rather than who has the most pressing needs or the best potential for success, you may create an environment where employees feel like they're in competition with each other. This can lead to resentment, low morale, and even sabotage.

4. You may damage your reputation.

If you're known for making reckless decisions, you may struggle to attract top talent or win the trust of clients and customers. This can ultimately harm your brand and your ability to succeed in the long term.

How to Avoid the Lottery Mentality

So, what can you do to avoid falling into the trap of a lottery mentality? Here are a few tips:

1. Gather data and do your research.

Before making any major decision, take the time to gather as much information as possible. Look at data, talk to experts, and get feedback from your team. This will help you make a more informed decision and reduce the element of chance.

2. Set clear goals and metrics.

Make sure you have a clear understanding of what success looks like before you invest resources or make a hire. Set specific goals and metrics that you can use to evaluate your progress and make adjustments as needed.

3. Be open to feedback.

Encourage your team to share their thoughts and ideas with you. Listen to feedback and be willing to adjust your approach if necessary. This will help you avoid the pitfalls of groupthink and make more well-rounded decisions.

4. Embrace a growth mindset.

Instead of relying on chance, look for opportunities to learn and grow. Encourage your team to do the same. This will help you stay adaptable and resilient in the face of challenges.

Conclusion

Managing with a lottery mentality can have serious consequences for both you and your team. By taking a more data-driven and intentional approach, you can avoid these pitfalls and build a more successful and sustainable workplace culture.

Don't miss out!

Visit the website below and you can sign up to receive emails whenever David C. Wyld publishes a new book. There's no charge and no obligation.

https://books2read.com/r/B-A-AOQKB-NFQHD

BOOKS2READ

Connecting independent readers to independent writers.

Also by David C. Wyld

Management 101
Management 101: Managing for Our Times

Watch for more at https://www.linkedin.com/in/david-wyld-4923707/.

About the Author

David C. Wyld currently serves as the Merritt Professor of Management at Southeastern Louisiana University in Hammond, Louisiana.

Read more at https://www.linkedin.com/in/david-wyld-4923707/.